"An enjoyable, compelling, an
next generation of camp leade
Christian camp literature."

— KIRK POTTER, Chairman, Fellowship of Christian Camps – BC;
Director, The Firs Retreat Center

"I am convinced this is a leadership resource that camp staff will
actually read. Craig writes with humour, charm, wisdom, conviction,
and a foundation that is built upon Scripture. This is a fantastic
contribution."

— JON MORRISON, Christian apologist, author, speaker, pastor,
podcast host

"In Lencioni-like fashion, Craig Douglas deftly weaves together
compelling narrative and timely leadership lessons that combine to
attract and engage the reader – as well as feed the soul. As insightful
and fun to read as it is, *Pillow Fights and Sleepless Nights: Thriving as a
Christian Camp Leader* is sure to be a major asset to any Christian Camp
summer training program."

— ROB THESSEN, Director, Camp Squeah

"Along with engaging stories, each chapter also provides wisdom,
challenge, and the heart of camp ministry as Craig shares his insights
and passion. This is a must read if you want to take your role in camp
ministry to the next level."

— RIKK KIEFT, Director, Gardom Lake Bible Camp & Retreat Centre

"After my 25 years in camping ministry, finally there is a clear guide
for any leader whether new or veteran. Craig has put into words what
my mentors have been saying all along."

— RYAN FRIESEN, former camp director

"I can't imagine a book that is more inspiring, practical, engaging and convicting for those working in camp ministry. Craig's heart for kids and for the Lord is evident on every page and his realistic approach to leadership development is right on target. I expect this to become standard reading for anyone working in camps, and for the weary leader needing to regain a vision and renewed energy for transforming lives through camp ministry."

— DR. TOM BLACKABY, best-selling author, international speaker, pastor

"This book excellently illustrates the ups and downs of camp-counselling, the laughter, the tears, and the many struggles that come with them. It offers sound, scripture-based teaching to help camp staff grow in their faith, rely on God, and make it through in one piece."

— LAURA THORNTON, author and camp enthusiast

Pillow Fights
&
Sleepless Nights

Thriving as a Christian Camp Leader

Craig W. Douglas

Pillow Fights & Sleepless Nights: Thriving as a Christian Camp Leader

William-Barnes Publishing
Maple Ridge, BC
Canada

Cover design by sam_4321 at fiverr.com.
Photo purchased from shutterstock.com.

ISBN: 978-1-7752490-0-9
eISBN: 978-1-7752490-1-6

Unless otherwise noted, all Scripture quotations are from Holy Bible, New Living Translation, copyright © 1996, 2004, 2015 by Tyndale House Foundation. Used by permission of Tyndale House Publishers Inc., Carol Stream, Illinois 60188. All rights reserved.

FOR...

Leanne, Ben, & Lorelle

You inspire me to live my life for Jesus, and you encourage me to write, in spite of all my insecurities and short-comings.

ACKNOWLEDGMENTS

Thank-you to the hundreds of leadership training students I have been privileged to teach and disciple over the past 30 years – you taught me more than I could ever teach you.

Thank you to Camp Qwanoes, for being instrumental in my spiritual growth and development throughout my younger years.

Thank you to Timberline Ranch, for teaching me my "grown-up" understanding of camp ministry, and for allowing me opportunities to hone my leadership training skills and knowledge.

Thank you to the many who read over this manuscript and gave me suggested improvements, especially my wonderful wife, Leanne, with her patient editing and marvelous formatting skills.

CONTENTS

INTRODUCTION

D ON'T DO IT, Jon!"
"Seriously, dude, this is a bad idea!"
"If we get caught, we are *so* dead!"
"*We* nothing. *We're* just watching, right?"

Jon smirked in the direction of his three co-conspirators and continued preparing his little joke. This was going to be hilarious, a trick he'd heard about at Bible College. Just fill the paper bag with shaving cream, put the open end under a door, jump on the bag, and *presto*! An indoor snowstorm! Hopefully, it wouldn't affect any computers in the camp program office, but he was fairly certain it wouldn't harm them.

"If you guys would keep it down, we might actually get away with this. Who wants the honors?" Jon indicated for someone to step up and jump on the bag. Carlos and Mike looked at Dave; Dave frowned and shook his head.

"No takers? Well, I guess it's up to me!" Jon chuckled quietly as he stood up. The others backed off a few steps. He took a deep breath, jumped in the air, landed both feet square on the bag, and *BOOM*!

The three observers felt a sudden wind and were instantly covered in fragrant, white, moist material. Sputtering and angry, Dave glared at Jon and exclaimed, much too loudly, "You *idiot*!"

Jon looked around, stunned for a moment, like he couldn't quite figure out what had happened, and then he started laughing. "You guys should see yourselves! Wow, that's not what I expected... Faulty bag, I guess!"

Dave found it a lot less funny and showed his displeasure. "That was brilliant, just brilliant, you moron! Why do we ever listen to you?!"

Jon laughed, "Because I'm a natural leader, and you boneheads need someone to show you how to have fun!" He cocked his head like he heard something and quickly added, "Let's get out of here. And maybe go wash off – you guys look ridiculous."

Carlos and Mike glanced around fearfully and then followed Dave as he quickly melted into the darkness, away from the program office lights. Jon suppressed another laugh as he grabbed the soggy remains of the bag. It was the first night of staff training, and this was going to be a great summer!

WELCOME TO CAMP: the most amazing and unpredictable place in the world, where God transforms lives and where young adults are given the opportunity to serve and to develop their leadership skills in all sorts of unique ways. If you are considering working at camp this coming summer, you are in for one of the greatest roller coaster rides anywhere. I won't promise it's going to be easy, but you will almost certainly learn and grow in ways you never expected.

I've often asked prospective camp workers, "Do you see yourself as a leader or as a follower?"

Almost invariably, they think the "right" answer is to say "Leader," though a few "hedge their bets" a little and say they are hoping to *become* a leader. In this age of individualism and self-focus, very few people want to admit to being a follower. Most people want to be those whom others will follow.

But understand this: the best leaders are *also* great followers. They are willing to submit themselves to God and to the leadership in place. I don't want to hire so-called "leaders" who won't follow instructions or obey the rules set out by our organization. This applies to everyone, including me. As the director of a camp, I still need to submit to my board of directors. Even if I had no board, being a follower of Jesus means I still, always, in *every* circumstance, have Someone to follow.

If you're reading this book right now, my guess is it's for one of two main reasons. Either you've been assigned this reading, or you truly want to become a great leader. Maybe it's a combination of the two. But if you want to become a great leader (or even an adequate leader – yes, dream big!), you'll need to submit yourself to learning from others who have a good idea as to how a good leader should look. That is what a "disciple" is: someone who follows and learns from another who has more experience than they have.

I'm not claiming to be an expert on leadership; in fact, there are times when I feel woefully inadequate to lead the mid-size camp I direct. However, I've had the opportunity over the past 30 years or so to train hundreds of young people who have taught me a lot about leadership. I have also been privileged to work alongside some great leaders who strongly exemplified good principles of leadership.

The style of this book may be somewhat different than you are used to. I will tell a fictional story about two leaders and their friends, who look and act like a lot of leaders I've encountered over the years. Read carefully, and from their choices, actions, thoughts, and consequences, you will see what good leaders do – and shouldn't do! After each section of the story, I will point out some things that can be learned from the story and give you some further discussion questions to consider.

As stated, the characters presented here are fictional. If you know me well or know my setting, you may be tempted to guess who is being represented by each character. Don't do it! I will deny everything! There are no specific circumstances recorded here. But on the other hand, our lives are made full by the people with whom we engage, so certainly anything of value here has been learned through interactions, and I am grateful for each one who has influenced my life over these past years in camp and youth ministry.

Oh, and the shaving cream gag? It rarely works, and if it does, it makes a real mess and makes people rather upset. My one encounter with it was someone who tried it on my dorm room at college – and it failed miserably. Actually, from my perspective, it failed *brilliantly*! I was in my room, heard a big "pop," and then heard a surprised yell, followed by running down the hallway. Outside my door was a mess, with an outline on the wall, in shaving cream, of a person who was presumably now covered in the stuff.

If, after reading this book, you think such pranks are appropriate for a camp environment or for good leaders, I will have failed in my goal to teach you leadership skills. And you will deserve to be covered in shaving cream.

GETTING READY FOR CAMP

CHAPTER 1

Feeling Like a Wart
Spiritual Gifts and the Body

"MADDY, WAKE UP! You're going to miss staff meeting!"
Already? It can't be much past 9:00 yet. Madison forced her eyes into the open position, then shut them immediately as the bright morning light pierced her skull. *Or earlier!*

"Maddy, come on! We're not allowed to be late!" Jen grabbed the blankets heaped over Madison and flung them to the side. "You've got like five minutes!"

"Wha' time is it?" Madison croaked, her mouth and throat bone-dry. She gave a small shiver as the cool air invaded her previously warm skin, and she pulled the covers back over herself.

"6:55. *Hurry up!*"

Madison forced her body into a slightly less horizontal position, leaning up on her elbows. *Camp. I'm at camp. Right. Okay. 6:55? Meeting at 7:00? What are they trying to do to us?* "I really gotta pee."

"Then *go!* I'll meet you in the chapel."

Madison arrived in the dimly lit chapel at precisely 7:02, and the meeting had already begun. *What is wrong with these people? We haven't even had breakfast! Do we really need a meeting already? Oh, great, it's Bruce. I hope he doesn't drone on and on again.*

She tuned into the director's nasally voice: "...and whoever sprayed shaving cream over by the program office last night needs to go and clean that up, please, *this* morning, *before* breakfast. Remember our policy on practical jokes. Really, people? I hope I don't have to say any more about this!"

It wasn't even that Bruce had nothing good to say, but he tended to be long-winded, and his voice grated on her a bit. Madison didn't have much patience for old people who talked too much.

Bruce finally introduced the morning's speaker. "Now then, I'm so glad to have Charlotte sharing with us this morning. I knew Charlotte when she was a camper, what, about 7 or 8 years ago? And here she is, tons of camp leadership experience under her belt, and she's our Head Cabin Leader this year. Let me pray for you, Charlotte."

He folded his well-weathered hands and closed his eyes. "Gracious Heavenly Father, please speak to us this morning through your Word, and give Charlotte your wisdom and strength to tell us what you have placed upon her heart. In Jesus' name, we pray, amen."

Bruce moved aside and sat down, while a short, slim lady with straight black hair stood up and went to the podium. *Isn't she cute?* thought Madison. *No wonder she's Head Cabin Leader. I'm too much of a slob to be hired for that kind of position.*

"Good morning, everyone! So glad to be here again this summer!" *Oh great, and she's perky. At 7:00 in the morning...*

Charlotte continued, her eyes shining with sincerity. "I was just thinking last night how much I miss this place the rest of the year, and how I get that feeling, you know *that feeling*, when I drive down that last bit of road before getting to camp. This place is like a home to me."

Madison glanced around and could see people nodding and then realized she was also nodding in agreement. Sure, she knew that feeling. In many ways, Crystal Lake Bible Camp was the home she never really had growing up.

Charlotte's smile lit up her face, and she continued, "Which, I guess, makes you all my *family* in the true sense of the word. Over the next couple of months, we're going to need to work together and depend on each other for support, encouragement, and practical help. This isn't the place to try to make it on your own! I'm so glad I have each one of you to watch my back, and I promise, to the best of my ability, and with God's help, I will be there for you this summer as well."

Really? wondered Madison. *I doubt you'll even notice me this summer. I'm not one of the popular friends you hang with.* In her heart, she knew she wished she was, though.

"Let's look at what God's Word says about the family of God in 1 Corinthians 12. Paul is explaining how each one of us has different spiritual gifts we all need to use to serve Jesus. Look what he says in verses 4-7. I'm reading from the *New Living Translation.*"

Madison saw that most people had their Bibles and were turning in them to the passage, but in her hurry, she'd forgotten her Bible. *Like I even know where 1 Corinthians is. At least this way nobody will notice me looking it up in the Table of Contents.*

As Charlotte began to read, Madison noticed her voice seemed to change. There was a quality in her tone that had a kind of *reverence* to it: "'There are different kinds of spiritual gifts, but the same Spirit is the source of them all. There are different kinds of service, but we serve the same Lord. God works in different ways, but it is the same God who does the work in all of us. A spiritual gift is given to each of us so we can help each other.'"

The voice changed back again as Charlotte looked up from her Bible. "Now hopefully you all know a little bit about spiritual gifts. I don't want to get bogged down on what gifts you might have and all that, but the point here is that above and beyond our natural abilities, the Holy Spirit, God, gives all of us Christians certain new abilities. These are specifically to be used to serve Him in the ministry of the gospel, both to other believers and to non-believers."

Spiritual gifts? Madison thought about it for a moment. Yeah, she'd heard that mentioned before, but she had no clue what hers might be. *Is messing up a spiritual gift?*

Charlotte looked down at her notes and then looked up and continued. "You might be good at soccer, for example, and that's something you either were born with, or you just learned really well. But God might also give you the *supernatural* gift of service, which means wherever you are, in church, camp, or even on the soccer field, you look out for the needs of others and help people. And, you probably feel happy and fulfilled whenever you can do that."

Sorry, but I'm not feeling happy or fulfilled about anything at 7:00 in the morning...

"The point is, these gifts are all from the same God, for His purposes, and they should unite us. Although we have different gifts, or different mixes of gifts, they are all for the same goal, to see the work of Jesus done wherever Christians gather together. So, at camp, that means we're all using our gifts to help kids discover Jesus and what He's done for them. We all work in different areas, like waterfront, or kitchen, or maintenance, or counseling, but as we serve faithfully, where we are, using the gifts and talents He has given us, the work gets done, and kids come to know Jesus and get transformed by Him."

Madison couldn't help but hang onto every word Charlotte spoke. Though hard to admit, Charlotte was very much the kind of person Madison wished she was. She spoke so sincerely, like she genuinely believed what the Bible said. No, it was more than that. *I believe the Bible is true. It just doesn't always seem relevant to me. It's just so old and* historical *or something.* But Charlotte didn't just act like it was true, she treated it like it genuinely *mattered.* Like she believed these were God's words for today.

"...describes us like a body. He says, starting in verse 12, that just like a human body, the body of believers – in a church or in a camp, or wherever they gather – has many parts that make up that one body. These all need to work together. He says, first of all, that nobody can say they aren't part of the body because they are just one specific part. So, if you're a foot, you can't say, 'well, since I'm not a hand, I certainly don't belong to the body.' Or 'I'm just an ear, I'm not important because I'm not an eye.'"

I'm a toenail. Or maybe a loose eyelash.

"Just imagine if someone here on housekeeping decided tomorrow that he or she wasn't important to this body, so they stopped cleaning the bathrooms. For a whole week. Can you imagine?"

Some of the guys at the back were laughing at some private joke, probably involving something disgusting in their bathroom. "Laugh it up, you guys," Charlotte quipped, "But I've seen your bathrooms, and they're nothing to be proud of!" Some of the girls laughed at that.

"But seriously, we're all *one* body, and we know that if anything isn't functioning well on our human body, the rest of the body suffers. Ever had an ingrown toenail? Or even a small wart or cut on the bottom of your foot? *One* tiny part is not working properly, and the *whole* body suffers."

That's me! I'm a wart!

"In fact, that's what Paul says in verse 26: 'If one part suffers, all the parts suffer with it, and if one part is honored, all the parts are glad.' So, all of us are vital to this body, and we all need to do what God has called us to do."

Madison had to think about that one for a while. *Is that true? Am I really needed here? Has God really given me gifts and abilities that will make a difference this summer? I sure hope so.*

"But the passage not only warns against this inferiority complex, which says *I'm only* . . . You fill in the blank. But it also says we have to be careful not to look at our gifts and abilities and become arrogant. Verses 21-22 say, 'The eye can never say to the hand, 'I don't need you.' The head can't say to the feet, 'I don't need you.' In fact, some parts of the body that seem weakest and least important are, in fact, the most necessary.'

"There are two warnings here. One danger is to think we're not needed or not important, but the second one is to make sure we never look at someone else and think *they* aren't needed. Hey, guys, we *need* each other this summer! I believe God has brought each one of you here for His purposes. No matter what circumstances brought you here, remember that it was not an accident, but part of God's sovereign plan for this summer. And for your life."

I really want to believe that's true, Lord. Have you truly brought me here for Your purposes?

"So, we need to bring our gifts, bring ourselves, and lay them on the altar as living sacrifices to Jesus, so He can use them to accomplish whatever He wants with you. It's going to be hard, but it's going to be worth it all, because God promises a little further on, in 1 Corinthians 15:58, 'Always work enthusiastically for the Lord, for you know that nothing you do for the Lord is ever useless.'

"Your service here at camp is not useless; it's not in vain, and it's not wasted. God will use it to accomplish His purposes. So be encouraged! What we're doing this summer is worthwhile! Let's pray."

Madison barely heard Charlotte's prayer, as her racing mind was considering all she'd heard this morning. *Not bad for 7:00 in the morning,* was Madison's fleeting thought at how awake she suddenly had become. *But if what she says is true, then maybe there is a point for me being here this summer. Maybe it doesn't matter that I have no abilities and no experience. God, can you really use me? That would be amazing. I don't want just to be a wart, Lord!*

Debriefing

OVER THE YEARS, I've seen a lot of different leaders come and go. First impressions are important, and I have done enough interviews to get a pretty good sense of what a person is going to be like if we hire that person.

But I've also been completely wrong. I think of Melanie, a popular college student with tons going for her in terms of abilities and personality. She started out great, but when things began to get hard, she became very prickly and sarcastic. It was soon clear that none of the other leaders liked her very much, and she was becoming ineffective with the kids. A girl I thought was going to be amazing was, in fact, rather ineffective.

I have to sorrowfully admit, to my shame, that I was fooled more than once by charisma, self-confidence, and even good looks. Aren't you glad that while *we* tend to look at outward appearances, *God* looks at and knows our hearts? In 1 Samuel 16:7, Samuel, the man of God, made the same mistake when looking for a king. In our story, this natural inclination of evaluating people based on appearances is an ongoing problem for numerous characters, including Jon and Madison.

I also think about several leaders we took on who seemed, on the surface, shy and insecure. Paul, for example, could hardly look me in the eye or talk to me when I met him. I thought, "These kids are going to walk all over him if we let him serve in a cabin!" But, against my better judgment, he was hired, and it was one of the best decisions we made that year. Paul was quiet and calm, but the kids loved him, and he connected well with them. Over time, he became a very effective leader.

The truth is, different campers connect with different kinds of leaders, so we need people with a good variety of personalities, experiences, and backgrounds.

We all want the "Charlottes" on our team, but if you knew her history, and what she went through to get where she is today, you might be surprised what she was like when she started working at camp. That's a different story that will only be touched briefly here.

And just as I have seen shy, insecure people become great leaders, I have also seen seemingly great leaders fail miserably because of poor choices they made. More leaders fail from *character issues* than from any lack of ability. So, your abilities are no guarantee you will be successful, nor are your inabilities any indication you won't be successful. What, then, makes a great leader? Keep reading, and that's bound to come up somewhere along the way…

The biblical illustration of the body and its members is helpful. We're not all alike, but we can all contribute. We need to celebrate diversity and stop trying to make everyone like ourselves. The goal is "unity in diversity" not "unity in sameness." By the way, that's where the word "university" comes from: a *diversity* of disciplines *unified* in the same location. We are all supposed to be different, and I am so thankful that no one on my staff is like me! They each have skills, knowledge, experiences, ideas, and preferences that are different than mine. I need them, and they need me. Most importantly, God has called each of us to serve Him the best we can with whatever He's given us.

I've introduced you, briefly, to two leaders, Jon and Madison, who are working at camp and who are going to be our primary examples of what good – and bad – leadership looks like. And there will be others, like the Director, Bruce, and the Head Cabin Leader, Charlotte, who will help us explore what it means to learn and lead and grow. Hopefully, you will be able to identify with some of them, and their experiences will help you become the leader and follower of Jesus that you were created to be.

Discussion Questions

1. Why do you think some camps are so strict about their leaders attending meetings and being there on time?

2. Which part(s) might represent your contributions to the body from the list below?

   - Hands – hard working, steady
   - Eyes – insightful, quietly helping people keep on task
   - Ears – patient, good listener
   - Feet – always on the go, always doing something
   - Heart – caring for those around you
   - Stomach – quietly taking it all in, strengthening the body however you can
   - Mouth – using words to help others along
   - Skin –holding everyone together, keeping the peace
   - Wart – firmly attached to the body but doing more harm than good
   - Hat – an accessory to the body, trying to look like you belong
   - Couch – not part of the body and doing your own thing
   - Wasp – not part of the body and dangerous to any part you encounter

3. Notice that the BRAIN isn't one of your choices, though you may think that's your gift! This is because the Bible says Jesus Himself is the Head of the body (see Colossians 1:18; 2:19). All the other parts of the body depend on *Jesus* for direction and coordination. What are the implications of that?

4. What happens when parts of a body don't connect properly with the Brain?

5. What happens when leaders at camp or in the church don't listen to Jesus? Can you think of a time when that was you?

6. Spiritual gifts are given to help the whole body accomplish God's mission in the world to draw people to Himself. How can you use

your gifts, wherever you are serving God (camp, school, work, church, among friends), to help accomplish this goal? How can people around you help you with that?

7. Are you ever guilty of assessing someone's worth or ability based on their appearances? Why is that unhelpful? How do you want others to decide what you are truly like?

CHAPTER 2

I Didn't Do It!
Influence & Character

H EY, JON, can we get on with this?"
Jon looked down from the climbing wall, as he held on with one hand. "I'm just demonstrating the proper way to do the overhang, *Justin.*"

Everyone laughed, and Justin turned red. *What a jerk*, Justin thought bitterly. *He's been up there showing off for ages.* "Ooh, look at me, I'm so amazing."

Jon gracefully leaped away from the wall, and with one bounce off the wall halfway down, he finished his descent and landed lightly on his feet. "All right, Justin, maybe you want to show us how it's done?" A few people looked toward Justin, but most people were a little embarrassed for him and avoided making eye contact. A couple of guys gave out short laughs.

Justin shook his head and kept his mouth shut. It was obvious to everyone that with Justin's larger size and lack of athleticism, he wasn't going to be demonstrating difficult climbs to anyone. He regretted speaking out, but he was so tired of Jon's antics, and it sure wasn't fair the way everyone let him do whatever he wanted. This session was *supposed* to be about how to safely set up the climbing wall and belay campers, not how to adore Jon's wonderful abilities.

As Jon began to explain further what he had done on the wall and why it was important for everyone to know how to belay kids who were on the overhang, Justin felt someone touch him on his shoulder from behind. He glanced back and saw Madison standing there with a sympathetic look on her face. "Don't worry about it, Justin," she said. "He's not trying to be nasty. He just wants us to be ready for the kids."

Justin half-turned to face her and muttered, "Why does everyone have to make excuses for him?"

"But I'm not. I'm just… Well, yeah, maybe I am. I don't know. He's a good guy, and he doesn't mean to make you feel bad. But, yeah, sometimes he comes across that way. I'm sorry."

Justin's shoulders slumped a little. "That's okay. I guess I'm probably a little jealous. I just hate how he's so good at everything, and then he has to…"

"…Make sure everyone knows it. Yeah, you're right. I'm sorry."

"Thanks, Maddy."

Madison grinned and gave him a little punch on the arm. "Hey, what are friends for? Don't let it get you down."

Uh, oh, I don't think I should've had that second taco. I am so stuffed.

Madison was pleasantly surprised at how good the food had been, and she was finding herself eating more than usual, justifying it with how busy they were being kept. *I'm going to have to have a little more self-control this summer, or I'm going to gain 20 pounds! Who would've guessed camp food could be so good?*

She wiped her hands on a paper napkin and got up from her chair. The next session began in ten minutes, and everyone from her table had already taken off. A couple of people hadn't put their plates away. The table was covered with bits of meat, lettuce, and various other things.

Although she was tempted to leave the mess for someone else to deal with (*I really need to go get ready*), Madison quickly gathered the plates and cups that had been left behind, placed them in the appropriate bins, and then grabbed a cloth. She wiped up the table, threw the cloth in the bucket, and looked at her watch. *Okay, I've still got 7 minutes. No problem.*

It was natural for Madison to clean up after other people, and she thought little of it. But it made a difference to the kitchen staff, who often felt unappreciated after cooking up a meal and seeing staff leave extra messes for them to deal with. And it influenced Josh, who came back to a different table to grab his hat, saw Madison cleaning up for others, and decided to do a better job cleaning his table after the next meal. And it encouraged Matt, the Head Maintenance Worker, who noticed it from across the room. He was tired of feeling ignored when reminding staff to clean up after themselves.

Jon walked into the Program Office without knocking and saw Charlotte at her desk, working on something on her computer. "How's it going, Charlotte? May I say you're looking great today?"

Charlotte looked at him quizzically and paused before choosing her words carefully. "Actually, Jon, I'd prefer if you didn't comment on my looks one way or another. No offense. It just makes me a little uncomfortable."

Jon's swagger and confidence seemed to shrink for a moment, but then he quickly recovered and said, "Sure, whatever you say, *Your Majesty.*" He gave a low, sweeping bow, grabbed a nearby clipboard, and turned to leave.

"Oh, and Jon, Bruce was looking for you. He would like to see you in his office as soon as you're available."

"Sure, thanks."

Man, she's a tough one, Jon thought as he wandered up the path to the administration building. *Hot as can be, but a tough nut to crack. Ah, well, by mid-summer, she'll succumb to my charms. They always do. Well, sort of. I wonder what Bruce wants. Probably wants to thank me for leading the belaying class. I hope I'm not in trouble. Surely, he didn't find out about any of those little pranks. Man, I gotta get my act together and stop acting like such a jerk. It's okay; I'm cool. It's all good.*

As he walked into the main office, he flashed his big white smile to Denise, the Office Manager.

"Hello, Jon. And how can I help you today?"

Man, she's gotta be seventy. Wonder why Bruce keeps her around? Not for her looks, anyway! "Hello, Denise! You having a good day? You accomplishing lots for the Kingdom today?"

Denise gave a faint, tolerant smile. "It's going well, thank you, Jon. How can I help you?"

Man, she's not exactly friendly, is she? "Just looking for Bruce. Is he around?"

"I'll see." Denise picked up the phone and punched in a couple of digits. "Hi, Bruce, Jon is here to see you. Sure, will do." She turned once more to Jon. "He says you can go right in."

"Thanks." He wandered down the hallway to Bruce's immaculate office. "Hey, Bruce, what's up?"

"Oh, hi, Jon," Bruce said, swiveling in his seat to face Jon. "How's your day going?"

"Oh, great. Led a session on belaying this morning, and was at the 'bullying' session until a few minutes ago. Should be another great summer!"

"Sure, sure. Listen, Jon, I have to ask you, do you know anything about the underwear on the flagpole this morning?" Jon felt like his heart missed a beat. "There's been some concern that we're seeing a lot of practical jokes this year already, and, as you know, our policy says we don't tolerate them."

Another big smile. "Why would you ask *me*, Bruce? I mean, I wouldn't do that!" *Ha, he can't pin this one on me!*

"Well, it has been suggested that you may have had something to do with it. Did you do it?" Bruce rubbed his head like he had a headache.

"No, Sir, of course not. Honestly, it wasn't me. I've been good!" *Easy boy, you're fine.*

"Okay, I believe you, Jon. But tell me, do you *know* who did it?"

Jon thought quickly. "Well, let's put it this way, I think I have a pretty good idea." *Actually, I know exactly who did it, because I stole the underwear and gave it to him!*

Bruce exhaled a forceful sigh. "Jon, *were* you or were you *not* involved in this?"

"Look, honestly, like I said, I have a good idea who did it, and I'll go talk to them if you want. I mean, yeah, that's a pretty dumb thing to do. Kind of funny, but not a good example, especially at staff training, where we're supposed to be developing unity and stuff like that…"

"Yes, Jon, please talk to your buddies and let them know there's going to be trouble if something like this happens again." Bruce eyed Jon slowly. "You do understand *why* we don't allow pranks here, right?"

"Um, sure, it's because it can hurt our unity and break trust and stuff." *Good answer.*

"Yes, and even more importantly, it makes it hard for campers — and staff — to feel *safe* or *secure*. It is counter-productive in building relationships. What seems funny to one person can absolutely terrify another, depending on their background and past experiences. In my many years of camp work, I've seen more people upset about pranks than I've ever seen people find them funny. And certainly, practical jokes have never brought a team together. Do you understand what I'm saying?

"Yes, of course, and I'll let them know. That was in real bad taste." *Man, I need to get out of here. He's going into lecture mode.*

"But more important than any of that is the question of *character*, Jon. Whether people think pranks are good or bad, the real point here is that the leadership at the camp has said 'no pranks,' so anyone doing pranks is breaking the rules and rebelling against authority. It's a character issue."

"Sure, yeah, definitely. We need to have good character. All of us." *Blah, blah, blah, blah.*

But Bruce still wasn't done. "Jon, you're a talented young man. You've got the looks, you're athletic, you're smart, and pretty much everyone likes you, including the campers. You have *charisma*. When you stand up in front of a crowd, people listen to you. They want to be like you."

"Well, thank you, sir. I guess I am very fortunate in that." *Wait, where's he going with this? I feel a 'but' coming.*

Bruce's eye contact was making Jon feel very uncomfortable. "That puts you in a position of heavy, heavy responsibility. What you *do*, and what you *say*, will have a huge impact on our staff and our effectiveness as a team this summer. If you choose to ignore rules, you will encourage others to do the same. If you make fun of people, they will feel it deeply. If you have a bad attitude toward authority, others will, too."

Jon just stared straight ahead and nodded. He didn't know what to say, so he figured it was best to keep his mouth shut. *For a change.*

"But Jon, if you focus on our ministry to kids, if you encourage staff, if you actively support the camp leadership, your example will make all the difference, and this could be an amazing summer for everyone. You're a key leader, even though you don't have an official title, and we need you on our side. I really want you to think about this and pray about this and decide why you're here this summer. If you *are* here to serve God, I'm excited to see what He's going to do with you this summer. If not, well, I'm not sure what we'll do with you."

Jon took a long time before answering, and the silence hung in the air thickly. *What am I supposed to say?* He looked past Bruce to the bookshelf behind him. Finally, without changing his gaze, he forced himself to respond. "Yeah, okay, I hear what you're saying. I'll give that some good thought. Thanks for the pep talk. I, um, better go to the next session. It's already started."

Bruce sighed again, and the tension was broken. "Please think about it, Jon. And pray about it. You're so influential, and you could make such a positive difference."

"Yeah, I'll think about it, for sure. You said some great things there. Stuff to think and pray about. Can I go now?"

"Yes, of course. Have a good afternoon."

"Thanks, you too," Jon replied automatically.

He walked back out of the office and down the hallway, not even looking up at Denise as he walked by. *Well, that wasn't what I expected. Just one little joke, and now I'm to blame for everyone's problems? I had no idea I had that much influence. But they don't pay me enough if they expect me to be such a perfect leader. Ha, that's Charlotte's job! They're lucky to have me working here this summer. I could be somewhere else making a whole lot of money. Oh, God, you gotta help me with my attitude, or I'm not gonna make it...*

Debriefing

P EOPLE LIKE JON can "make or break" a ministry. If we don't have them on our side, we're in for a lot of grief and frustration. Here's something we need to understand:

> **Leadership is primarily influence; positive influence comes from good character.**

Let's break that down a bit. The traditional way to understand leadership was always "top-down." Someone is given the authority to lead, and because they have that authority, everyone lower down on the ladder does what they say. The person at the top is the leader, and everyone below them is a follower. Those at the bottom are not required to make decisions; they simply need to obey.

For example, at a camp, if the board tells the director to do something, she does it. If the director tells the maintenance manager to do something, he obeys. If the maintenance manager tells the housekeeper to do something, she makes it a priority, and if she tells a volunteer to do something, that volunteer also is expected to do what he is told. It's clean and simple. Anyone above you on the authority ladder leads you, and you lead anyone below you on the ladder. It can be frustrating to be on the bottom, but the hope is always that someday you can move up and start to make a difference.

But this model doesn't define true *leadership*; it only shows *authority* and lines of communication flowing to and from that authority. You can easily have someone with authority who doesn't lead well, just as you can have someone on the bottom of the totem pole who is a huge influence within the organization. Unless each employee or volunteer is empowered to make decisions and operate within their scope of responsibility, the organization will never succeed in the way it hopes to.

True leadership comes from *anyone* within an organization who understands the mission of the organization and influences others in the direction of that mission, regardless of their position or authority.

The big problem with a top-down authority leadership model is that this requires the assigned leaders to be on top of what everyone beneath them is doing, all the time. Yet people are most effective when they are trained to act and make decisions on their own. Even a soldier must be taught to think for himself when his sergeant isn't there with him, or when things start to get crazy, like in battle.

Another problem with this model of leadership is that it assumes that the person ultimately in charge knows everything going on within the organization. But in reality, the higher up you are in an organization, the harder it is for you to know what is going on where it matters the most.

For example, Bruce has no idea why there was underwear on the flagpole this morning. He happened to see it as he came to his office. His board, the leaders highest on the ladder, still don't know about it, and they probably never will. Bruce, upon seeing the underwear, inquires of his managers to see if they know about it. They don't know, but someone heard a rumor that Jon had something to do with it, which is a pretty good guess if nothing else.

Bruce, as director, decides to deal with it directly. He has authority, but he didn't have all the information he needed to deal with the current problem. Imagine if Bruce dealt with every problem in this way! He would never get done the important work only he can do. But in this case, he feels it is important to try to get an influencer within the organization (Jon) heading the right way, influencing people in the direction that is best for the camp's mission.

Top-down leadership, while important in terms of policy setting and communication, is generally ineffective in terms of helping the organization move forward in fulfilling its mission. That needs to come from others within the organization, wherever they have influence. Bruce recognizes this and goes after someone who he knows will be a key leader and influencer for good or for ill.

Think about it: if the mission of the camp is to draw campers to Jesus, who has the best opportunity to do this? Is it the director or the office staff, as they work through all the administration necessary to keep the organization running, or is it the volunteers who are on the front-line, working with the kids?

Not only do the front-line staff have the best opportunities to influence campers toward Jesus, but they also set the tone for the whole camp with how they treat one another. Compare Jon's not-so-subtle put-downs of Justin with Madison's encouragement of Justin. Which one of them was influencing Justin toward Jesus? Which one of them was encouraging unity in the body? Which one was leading positively? Whose actions were in line with the mission of the camp? Jon had more authority at the climbing wall, but Madison's actions were more effective in drawing someone to Jesus. So who was the better leader?

Good leadership can be simply defined as "positively influencing people in the right or best direction."

Sometimes leadership requires a person to be up front, *showing* people where to go, but more often it involves those within the ranks who are a positive influence to help people head in the right direction. Good leaders don't need titles or positions – they simply need to know where the organization is going and to be part of the process to help it get there. We call that *influence*, and we all have it to varying degrees wherever we go.

I often see this at staff training when it is time for people to get to a session, and people are sitting around chatting. I watch to see who it is who will break off conversations and head to the session so it can start on time. Their example will usually encourage others to do the same. Sometimes, someone will even outright say something like, "Five minutes until the next session," reminding their fellow staff members to get moving. They are good leaders – good influencers.

The danger with influence, of course, is that it can be used for good or evil. Think of someone you know who is constantly belittling people or putting down authority or doing things that make it hard to do what's important. They may be very influential, but their character is such that their influence is negative. They are influencing people in a direction, but not positively, and not in the direction they *should* go, according to the mission of the organization, or according to the will of our God.

This is why positive influence boils down to the *character* of the influencer. The person who is walking closely with Jesus is going to act in ways that draw people to Him, whereas people living for themselves will tend to do things, often inadvertently, like making an offhand comment, that move people away from Jesus. In a Christian organization that has a Christian mission, character plays a huge role. Anyone with genuine faith and a consistent life of obedience to Jesus will be able to make a huge, positive difference.

That's why the Apostle Paul could say to his readers, "you should imitate me, just as I imitate Christ" (1 Cor. 11:1). Here we see clearly his *influence* ("imitate me") and *character* ("as I imitate Christ"). In being close to Jesus, Paul's character was good enough that he could influence people in the ways of Jesus. That should be the goal of every believer. He needed no "position" in the church to do so.

> **You don't have to be in charge to lead through influence, but to lead well, you need to follow Jesus closely.**

Jon and Madison are both in positions to be influential, to make a difference, and as the story progresses, we will see this more and more. Keep noticing what they and others do to draw people *toward* or *away* from the mission of the camp, and ask yourself, what kind of leader will you be?

Discussion Questions

1. Have you ever seen a practical joke go sideways and hurt or offend people? Were you ever the victim?

2. Have you ever been hurt by someone's careless words? Have you hurt others with careless words? How?

3. When you think of a good leader, who do you think of, and why?

4. What are some qualities of leaders who have had a genuine influence on your life?

5. Why is a top-down leadership model mainly useful only for emergencies, communication, and setting policies?

6. Why does *influence* better define leadership than *authority*?

7. What is the connection between influence and character? What happens if someone has influence but bad character? Is it possible for someone to have good character but no influence?

8. What can we do if our character needs work? Do we need to be perfect to be a leader? If you were to set a minimum standard, what would you expect in a camp leader?

CHAPTER 3

Sticky Dishes & Religious Stuff
The Mission

THE SUN WAS SHINING, the grass was green, wildflowers were blooming on the edges of the fields, and a light breeze kept this early July day from being too hot. It was a perfect first day of camp.

The cabin leaders looked terrific in their blue and green staff T-shirts, and everyone could hear and feel the excited and anxious buzz of campers arriving by the car-load. Parents hovered over them, making sure they were going to be all right, that they remembered everything, and that they knew where the toilets were. There were some tearful goodbyes, but most everybody was happy and thrilled, either to be at camp or to be leaving a child there.

Jon looked at his clipboard. *Just one more camper to come. Hopefully, he'll be somewhat normal, not like that kid in the corner bunk. He's going to be a handful. Seriously, kid, get your finger out of your nose!*

As the other boys in the cabin noisily settled in and tried to figure out where to put their things, a short boy with bright red hair dragged his suitcase into the cabin, followed by a woman who must be his mother. She was taller than him, but not by much, and tattoos were evident pretty much anywhere skin was showing. She wore large, dark sunglasses, and the rest of her face had heavy make-up.

"Okay, Jimmy, you gonna be okay?" Her raspy voice sounded like she was probably a heavy smoker.

"Yeah, mom, I'm *fine*. You can go now." Jim glanced nervously around at the other boys, trying not to look like an idiot in front of them.

Behind the sunglasses, the eyes flashed angrily. "I'll go when I'm ready to go. Did you pay for this camp, or did I?" The cabin went silent. She looked over at Jon. "You the cabin leader?"

Jon looked up. "Yeah, ma'am, that's me. I'm Jon." He held out his hand, which the woman ignored.

"Whatever. Listen, we're *atheists*, and we don't want any religion this week, okay?"

Jon didn't know what to say. "Um, I'll see what I can do."

"No, you need to do better than that. I had friends whose kids came here, and they were brain-washed. Jimmy doesn't need that."

Jon shifted uncomfortably where he stood. "Well, you'd better talk to the director, because this is a Christian camp, you know."

The lady raised her eyebrows, and removed her sunglasses, revealing piercing eyes and dark, drawn-on eyebrows. "Oh, I will." She turned back to her son, who was putting his sleeping bag on the lower bunk by the door. "Jimmy, you be good. See you in a week." She went over to him and hugged him gently from behind, a gesture Jimmy didn't try to return.

Jon held the clipboard toward the lady and offered his pen. "Can you please sign Jimmy in and let us know if anyone else will be picking him up?" Without a word, she scribbled her signature and handed the pen back to Jon.

As she exited the cabin, she looked back at Jimmy and pointed at him. "Be good."

As soon as she left the cabin, the other boys started talking again, like nothing had happened. Jimmy turned around and looked at them, wondering if he would be able to make friends now that they had seen his mom be such a jerk. He saw Jon looking at him and nodded toward him. "Hey."

"Welcome to my cabin, Jimmy. I'm Jon. This your first year?"

"Yeah. Call me Jim. And don't worry about my mom. She's just like that."

"That's okay."

"I don't care about the religious stuff. It's fine. It doesn't bother me like it bugs my mom."

"Well, that's good. Don't worry, other than chapel and praying at meals, it won't be too bad. I'm supposed to do some Bible study stuff with you guys, but we're usually too tired in the evenings to do much. It'll be cool."

"Okay." Jim went back to his unpacking.

Well, the kids had all arrived, and the week had begun. Jon surveyed his small kingdom and decided it was time to bring them together. "Okay, guys, five minutes to finish what you're doing, and then we're going to go have some fun."

Daniel, a lanky 12-year-old, looked up at Jon, and asked, "What are we doing? It better not be lame."

Jon smiled mysteriously. "Oh, you'll see. Come on you guys, finish up and let's go!"

"Here, have some *more!*"

Madison groaned as Jennifer pushed another stack of sticky plates through the service window. It felt like she had been washing dishes forever, but it was only 8:20 a.m., and she had been at it for less than an hour.

The week of staff training had been great. Despite the early mornings and long days, Madison had enjoyed getting to know other staff members, learning how to lead in different areas, listening to speakers passionately talk about Jesus and how to teach campers about Him, and singing the camp songs. Even the daily chores weren't bad. She had been so excited for opening day when the campers would come, and she could finally start working with them and showing God's love to them.

That was until Friday, the last day of staff training. The news came from Charlotte.

"Hey, Maddy, can I talk to you for a minute?"

"Sure." *Uh-oh. Well, at least she knows my name.*

"Listen, I just wanted to let you know we have several people who canceled on us for the kitchen this week, and we're going to have to put you in there. Just for this week, and then you'll be in the cabin with campers next week. I hope that's okay?"

"Yeah, sure, wherever I can help." *No! Seriously? That's the last place I want to be!*

"Thanks, Maddy! I told Bruce you'd be okay with it since I really see a servant's heart in you! Thanks for being so flexible and doing whatever it takes to serve Jesus this summer."

And so here she was, stuck in the kitchen with stacks of disgusting dishes, oozing with syrup and various unidentifiable food bits. *I came to work with kids, not dishes! This is so gross!*

"Hey, Madison, let me give you a hand with those." Jennifer came over, rolled up her sleeves, and started scrubbing one of the big porridge pots that had been soaking in the sink, flashing a smile at Madison that lit up her face. Madison continued to rinse plates and put them in the racks.

She's nice. A little too cheerful, but nice.

"So, they recruited you for the kitchen, hey?" Jennifer asked as she scraped the pot. "I heard we were going to be short without you, so thanks for stepping up for us!"

"Well, it wasn't really my choice. I was kind of planning on working with kids this summer, so, well, yeah." She looked up at Jennifer for a split second and managed to spray herself, as the water did a reverse in a bowl back onto her apron. "Arg! I'll never get the hang of this!"

Jennifer laughed. "You're doing fine! I usually manage to soak myself at some point most days, and I've been doing this for years!"

"But why the kitchen? Don't you want to work with the kids?"

Jennifer thought for a moment, while she continued to scrub the pot. "Well, the way I see it, it doesn't matter where I serve, as long as I give my best to the Lord. I mean, if nobody works in the kitchen, how are the campers going to eat? And if they don't eat, they won't come, and if they don't come, how can they hear about Jesus? But if they do come and hear about Jesus, their lives can be changed, right?"

She's a lot deeper than I thought. "Sure, I can see that, but why *you*? You'd be great with kids. They'd love you as a cabin leader."

Jennifer again hesitated before answering. "Yeah, I've been in the cabin with the campers, and it was great, but fewer people want to work in the kitchen, so I try to come and volunteer here a couple of weeks every summer because I know how important it is. And besides, there are great people to work with in the kitchen, too. Like you, I'm thinking!"

Madison smiled, despite herself. "Aw, thanks. But do you really like cleaning up after everyone all the time and dealing with complaints and all that stuff? I've just started this morning, and I'm already sick of people's attitudes toward the kitchen staff!"

"Well, that's another reason to have everyone work in the kitchen once in a while – it makes us all appreciate what happens in here more." She lifted the pot out of the sink and emptied its contents. "But another reason I like being in the kitchen is that I get to talk to lots of the staff, and build into their lives a bit. Some of them are where I was at just a few years ago, and I think this is a great opportunity to help them through some of the things they're facing. I guess I see the kitchen as every bit as much of a mission field as working with the campers."

"Hmm, well, I guess I never thought of it that way. Even as a camper I thought the kitchen was just kind of like the *slaves* of the camp, while everyone else got to have fun."

Jennifer gave a wry grin. "Don't get me wrong, it's hard work, and I get pretty tired by the end of a shift. But even then, afterward, I get to hang out with staff and help with the evening game and go to campfires. So, I'm still with staff and campers most of the day, but without the responsibility of campers of my own. There are some good trade-offs working in the kitchen."

Madison pushed another rack of dishes into the dishwasher and started it up. "Yeah, I guess."

"Listen, Maddy, what I'm trying to say is that 'ministry' is wherever you are *right now*, to the people who are around you, *right now*. Some people study and 'train' for ministry for years and years and miss the opportunities that surround them every day. You don't have to look far to find people who are struggling, and at camp, that includes both staff and campers. So why not take each opportunity to speak truth and life into them? Why not love them and help them however you can?"

Madison nodded as she focused on carefully spraying the plates, keeping the water moving safely away from her.

Jennifer grabbed another pot and continued, "I'm here at camp because I believe in the mission, that we have the opportunity to make a real difference in people's lives. And if that means putting in long hours doing dishes or peeling vegetables, I'm okay with that because it means that campers – and staff – get to be here and learn about Jesus. Yeah, it's not always so glamorous," Jennifer said laughing, her arms in greasy water up to her elbows, "but it's important work, and I know that serving here is making a difference."

"Thanks, Jennifer. I probably needed to hear that. I was just feeling sorry for myself, but I have to remember it's not all about me, is it?"

"It's not *about* you, true, but you're still very important to the ministry here in the kitchen. And it'll be a fun week working with you. I'd better go get the cutlery," Jennifer said as she walked back into the Dining Hall.

Madison filled yet another rack of plates, her hands dripping and sticky. *Well, sure, I guess it's all for the kids, after all.* Then she straightened out and cracked her neck to one side. *Even more than that, it's for Jesus and His mission to this world. That Jennifer is no dummy. I need to talk with her more...*

Debriefing

I CAN'T EMPHASIZE ENOUGH how important it is to know and understand the mission of the camp or organization for which you work. In any kind of work, you need to know what the organization is trying to accomplish. This should be clear to everyone.

I'm not just talking about a vague "mission statement," though mission statements can be helpful. But if you are working somewhere, and you know the bottom line is to make *money* for the shareholders, that will help you know how to make decisions in your everyday work. You will understand, for instance, that good service is required primarily to gain repeat customers, not necessarily because the organization cares about people.

Similarly, if your organization exists to provide a *service*, then you will do everything you can to make the customer satisfied. Such companies still need to make money to pay their bills, but the driving force is service-oriented.

In Christian camp ministry, the bottom line should be "evangelism" and "discipleship." Most camps will tend to lean more heavily toward one or the other.

By *evangelism*, I mean proclaiming the gospel, the "good news" about Jesus Christ, how He came and died on a cross to pay for the sins of all people, conquering death through His resurrection, so that whoever puts their trust in Him will be "saved," gaining eternal life.

By *discipleship*, we generally refer to the next steps of people growing in their relationship to God, becoming more like Jesus Christ, and learning to use their spiritual gifts to serve God.

If I were to boil this down even further, I would say the purpose of evangelistic camps is this:

To provide opportunities for Jesus to transform lives.

In my mind, that's the bottom line. We want people to be saved (evangelism), and we want people to grow in their faith (discipleship), and that means both initial and continual *transformation*, with the ultimate goal to bring each person to maturity in Jesus Christ. Colossians 1:28-29 says:

> So we tell others about Christ, warning everyone and teaching everyone with all the wisdom God has given us. We want to present them to God, perfect in their relationship to Christ. That's why I work and struggle so hard, depending on Christ's mighty power that works within me.

If *transformation* to maturity (or becoming "perfect") in Christ is the overall mission or purpose of what we are doing, we need to be very deliberate in teaching the entire staff to know and understand that.

Do people working in maintenance understand that what they do contributes toward seeing campers and staff members transformed? How about in the kitchen, or in different program areas?

Do we see building into our staff and volunteers as key to our mission? Sometimes, it is so easy to focus on the campers that we neglect the opportunity we have with the adults in our ministry. I think it's easy to focus on them during training times and then just "release" them to do ministry, correcting them as need be, supporting them in their roles, but forgetting they are an integral part of our mission field. In fact, our opportunities with our staff and volunteers are often greater than those we have with the campers.

When children come to camp, what is the best thing we can do for them? When asking this question, I've heard people say, "Teach them about Jesus!" That's not a bad answer, as far as it goes, and teaching is of utmost importance. But how do we do that? As is often said, "Much more is caught than taught." In other words, people are learning all the time, usually more by what they see and experience than by what they are told. So, children at camp will *hopefully* learn some things from the speaker or the cabin leader, but they will *always* learn from what they experience.

At a Christian camp, what we want is children (and workers!) to have an amazing *experience* that draws them to Jesus – so that they can be transformed.

I believe that an amazing and beneficial experience at a Christian camp will primarily include four types of experiences:

1. Experiencing *Fun*

If you ask kids why they are going to camp, they'll almost always say it's for the great activities, the *fun*. Many camps have specialty activities like horseback riding or waterskiing or back-packing, and those are often what initially attract kids to a camp. Whatever the specialty or the activities at camp, it should be incredibly enjoyable, where kids can be kids, where they can try new activities, play great games, and be wild and crazy. Why would anyone go to a camp that isn't fun? Campers need to experience healthy doses of fun!

2. Experiencing *Growth*

When I talk to parents about camp, they say they want it to be a fun experience, but usually, they also hope their child will learn, grow, and develop while there. Camps have a unique opportunity to offer that as part of the experience, as children try new challenges, learn to socialize with other kids and adults that they live with, learn new skills, and receive good teaching. They develop confidence and can grow in mind, body, and spirit.

3. Experiencing *Community*

It has been interesting to me that a significant number of campers who come back in subsequent years, although they still talk about the fun times and maybe what they learned in past years, come back to camp because it has become their *community*, their home, their haven. They talk about how they find acceptance at camp they don't find anywhere else. They engage in teamwork, where they contribute their ideas or physical prowess or simple things like cleaning up after a meal or sweeping the cabin. They sit around campfires and sing together, and they engage in meaningful discussions in the cabin. They come back because, possibly like nowhere else, it's a place where people care for them, and they feel like they belong.

4. Experiencing *God*

Fun, growth, and community all help campers to be in the right place, in body, mind, and spirit, so that they are also able to experience God. In the midst of everything else going on, there should be time for quiet and contemplation and appreciation of the creation and the Creator. There should be space to think, ask questions, and then see the truth of those answers lived out in the lives and love of the staff. Camp may be the only place these campers have Christian role models who truly care for them. They may struggle and mess up, but even this helps the campers understand what the Christian life is like and how far the love and the forgiveness of God extends.

This is the amazing experience campers enjoy, the experience that, when extended to them by sincere believers, draws them to their Savior, Jesus Christ. The truth is, that's why I "do camp," and that's our mission: to see campers and the staff transformed by Jesus, becoming mature in their faith in Him.

Discussion Questions

1. At the beginning of this chapter, do you think Jon and Madison understood and embraced the purpose of the camp they work at? Explain.

2. What do you think is the mission of wherever you serve or work? How is this communicated? Would you say that this mission is consistently lived out by everyone? By the leaders?

3. Why do you think non-Christians send their kids to Christian camps? Do you think it's "brainwashing" to teach kids from the Bible? Why or why not?

4. How can we stay true to the gospel and yet avoid having non-Christian parents feel like their kids are being brainwashed?

5. How does each department of a camp contribute toward the mission? Is there any area that is more or less important than another area in regard to fulfilling the mission? Explain.

6. Do you agree with Jennifer that your "ministry is wherever you are, right now, to the people who are around you, right now"? What difference would that simple philosophy make if all Christians believed that and lived that way?

7. When you aren't at camp, what is your ministry? Or rather, who is your ministry outside of camp? What does that look like for you? What can you do to take advantage of the opportunities around you?

WORKING WITH CAMPERS

CHAPTER 4

What if They Hate Me?
Building Relationships

MADISON PACED NERVOUSLY between the bunk beds in her cabin. She was glad to have survived a week in the kitchen, and it was a lot more fun and fulfilling than she expected. In fact, she had to admit that she truly enjoyed the friendly banter with Jennifer and a number of the other workers, and although the work was hard at times, it was also pretty fun. And she had learned some new things, like making buns and laying out veggie platters. She also appreciated the freedom she had to help out in the evenings with the games and to get to know some of the campers, some of whom she'd even been able to sit with at campfire two nights in a row.

But this was a new week, and none of that was on her mind right now. In less than an hour, hordes of junior campers would descend upon the camp, and she would be responsible for eight little lives.

What if they hate me? What if they think I'm boring? What if they're all "girlie" and I'm too much of a tom-boy? And I just know I'm going to have a bed-wetter or two. How am I going to handle kids who talk back to me? What if I get mad and lose my cool? Ahhhhh. This is stupid. I should never have thought I could do this!

She looked over her cabin. It was neat, tidy, and nicely decorated with streamers and other supplies she'd picked up at the dollar store to try to make her cabin a little bit special for these 10 and 11-year-olds that she would be living with for the next week. But was it too much? Was it overdone? Would they think it was too childish? *Kids are so sophisticated these days, growing up too fast. I would have loved my cabin to look like this, but what if they hate it? Or mock it? Oh, I hope they get along with each other...*

"Hey, Maddy!" Madison glanced around, and there was Charlotte, smiling and poking her head into the cabin.

"Oh, hi, Charlotte. Here we go!"

"Nervous?"

"Who, me? Uhh, yeah, maybe a bit?" *Like completely freaked out of my mind.*

"Well, just remember, you don't have to do this alone."

"Yeah, I know. Jesus is right here beside me." Madison tried not make it sound "religious," but she felt like she needed more than just the invisible hand of God at that moment.

"No, I mean, well, yes, He is! But what I meant was that if you have any problems with your girls, I'll be around to give you a hand. And Lu and Sparks as well. But you're going to do great. Really. Okay?"

"Yeah, I'll be fine." *Or not. Why am I doing this?*

Charlotte observed her closely, walked in a few steps, sat on the edge of a bunk, and looked around. "Nice job with the cabin. Your girls are going to love it!"

"I hope so. Just hope they like me."

Charlotte looked into Madison's eyes with compassion. "It's your first time, right? I sure remember my first cabin. Thought I would fail miserably. Yeah, it was hard at times, and I learned things every time I counseled that gradually made me a better cabin leader, but even that first time went very well, in spite of all my fears of failure!"

"But that's you. Everyone likes you. When have you ever failed at anything?"

Charlotte stifled a laugh. "Oh, Maddy, you are so kind, but believe me, I've had plenty of failures and lots of fights with friends and roommates and family! What you see of me at camp isn't the whole story, believe me! If you only knew the insecurities I deal with on a daily basis!"

"*You*? I find that hard to believe."

Charlotte's face grew serious. "I don't talk about it a lot, but I've had some pretty serious issues to deal with over the years, including bulimia and alcoholism. I had some pretty dark years as a teenager."

"Really?" *Woah, didn't see that coming.*

"Look, Maddy, it isn't about being *perfect*. These campers don't need perfection; they just need you to be real and to love them, to spend time with them, to pay attention to them. You know all the stuff we covered in staff training about working with kids, but the main thing, the thing that makes all the difference in the world to them is that you *care* and that they know you care."

"But what if I *don't* care? What if I don't even *like* them? What if they sense that, and they . . . they hate me?" *Oh, great, now I'm gonna cry.*

"Maddy, as I've observed you over these past two weeks, the thing I've seen is that you genuinely care about people. In fact, I think the only thing stopping you from having more friends at camp is that you have a hard time letting people in. I was like that a few years ago, too. Maybe I'm still that way. But I've seen your compassion, I've seen you come alongside others who are struggling, I've seen you be a friend to other staff who aren't particularly popular and who needed a friend. When I started counseling, I had none of the compassion you have, and I'm pretty sure I was far more insecure than you are!"

"But I don't remember all the things you guys taught us at staff training. The kids are going to come, and my mind is going to go blank, and I'm going to mess up!" The tears welled up in her eyes, and Charlotte came over and wrapped her arms around her. Madison thought she smelled like vanilla and didn't mind it a bit.

"Trust me, Maddy, you're just nervous, like we all are when we lead a cabin. Not just the first time, either! It gets easier, but we always wonder how it's going to go until the kids show up, and then we're too busy connecting with the kids to worry about those things."

"Thanks, Charlotte. Sorry I'm such a nervous wreck."

Charlotte let go and gave Madison some space. "Just be there for them. Ask them questions about what they like. Do things *with* them. They will know you love them if you spend time with them. The rest will fall into place."

"Okay. Sorry, I'll be fine. It's just so new to me, and it kinda stresses me out a bit."

"And the reason you're stressed is because you *care*! Which is a good thing. Don't lose that. And believe me, I've seen a lot of rookie cabin leaders who don't have half the gifts and abilities to work with kids that you do, and most of them have done a fine job in spite of it. Oh, and yeah, as corny as it sounds, Jesus *is* right beside you! He's got this thing!"

"29-32-44 hut, *hut*." Sammy snapped the ball back between his legs and almost hit Jon in the face before Jon's quick reflexes allowed him to grab it.

"One steam-boat, two steam-boat, three steam-boat, four steam-boat, five steam-boat!" The last two were said in the space of less than a second, as three campers ran through and around the helpless blockers in front of Jon.

Jon laughed as they came at him, confident he could avoid their outstretched hands trying to tag him. Just as he looked like he would be caught, he planted his right foot, changed direction, and pulled his hips out of harm's way. Rolling to his left, he spotted Peter making a fast arc to the right, ahead of a chunky young lad trying to keep up with him. Jon released a perfect spiral and hit Peter on the run at chest-height. Peter stuck out his hands and made the catch, almost tripping as he did. As he regained his balance and looked upfield, he was tagged by another boy coming from downfield.

"Yeah! Peter! Great catch, buddy! First down!" *Perfect throw! Anyone could've caught that!*

One of the boys who had been trying to tag Jon before he threw the ball looked at Jon and said, "No fair! You're too fast! I *had* you!"

"That's okay, Trent, you'll probably get me next time. I'm getting too old for this. You did a nice job of getting around the blockers that time." *Man, I have terrible blockers!*

"Can I be on your team next game?"

"Well, maybe. We'll have to see what makes fair teams, right? If you and I play together, we'd probably be invincible, and then no one else would want to play."

Trent smiled at that thought. "Yeah, you're probably right. But I still think we should try it!"

Trent went back to his team as the rest of Jon's team came in for a huddle. "Nice one, Peter! Okay, next play, we're going to do a draw. Does anyone know what that means?"

"A run that looks like passing play?" One kid asked.

"Exactly. We'll set up like we're going to throw a short pass to Peter, who needs to go about ten yards and then cross to the right in front of me. He'll probably be covered better this time. You two guys go long. Morgan, you start over there and run behind me. I'll give the ball to you. The idea is to run up the middle wherever there's a gap, so we need *you* guys to block and make a gap. Any questions? Okay, let's do this thing!"

Despite Jon's somewhat adequate but hurried description of the play, it was doomed from the snap, which was low and almost bounced past Jon. He grabbed it, looked up, saw Peter running left instead of right, and pump-faked a pass to him. Then he turned to find Morgan . . . who wasn't there. As Jon scrambled backward to buy some time, he ran into and stumbled over Morgan who had shown up from his blind side, and he felt two hands smack him from behind.

"Gotcha!" Trent crowed. "For a *huge* loss! Ha, I knew it was just a matter of time! In. Your. Face!"

"Shut up, you moron." It was Morgan, who was getting up after being knocked over by Jon. "You guys suck."

The triumph on Trent's face drained immediately and was replaced by a scowl. "Shut up yourself, butthead. And learn how to walk, hey?"

Jon quickly intervened. "Hey, guys, chill. It's just a game. We're having fun." He looked at the two boys still scowling at each other. "Seriously, chill! Trent, nice job on the sack, and Morgan, sorry for running into you, man! I totally messed up that play!" *Yeah, like it was my fault! A little bigger, and I could've been in the NFL.*

Morgan looked at Jon gratefully, as Trent headed back to his team. "Yeah, sorry, I think I was in the wrong place. I don't play much football at home."

"But you're having fun, right?"

Morgan thought for a moment. "Yeah, it's okay. I prefer golf."

"You golf? Too cool. I am so bad at that game!" *Well, compared to most sports.* "You'll have to give me some tips sometime."

"Yeah, that would be great. I'll tell you about my *almost* hole-in-one a few weeks ago. Totally rimmed the hole!"

Everyone was gathering to huddle for the next play. "Okay, guys, that was a *perfect* example of how *not* to run a draw! Let's try something a *little* simpler this time..."

Debriefing

B UILDING A RELATIONSHIP with a camper is not that much different from building a relationship with a peer. It mainly requires an investment of time and patience. There are also some specific skills that anyone can learn and develop to become a better relator. The following suggestions are effective in any relationship, not only with a camper.

1. Use Names

One of the simplest tools to help you connect with campers quickly is to learn and use their names immediately. Some people are naturally skilled at this, and others have to work hard at it. The rule of thumb should be to know all your campers' names by the time the first meal is over. Use that first meal to go over their names. I always found reading over a list before they arrived helped a lot because then you just need to attach the names you already know to the faces. And when the kids aren't looking at you, grab your cheat sheet, and keep going over it until you've got it.

2. Make Eye Contact

Whenever you pass by campers you don't know, look them in the eye and smile at them. They will usually see that as a sign that you're friendly. Some kids and some cultures have trouble with eye contact, so be aware of that, but for most people, when the eye contact is natural (and people remember to blink occasionally), it shows you are interested in what they are doing and saying.

3. Initiate Conversations

Don't wait for campers to talk to you. Some will do that easily (and some will never stop talking to you), but in general, when you initiate a conversation, it is telling them you are interested in them and in their lives.

4. Avoid Smothering

We all need space sometimes, and campers are no different, especially the less extroverted ones. While it is vital to initiate, it is also vital to be sensitive to their need to be left alone at times. Don't take this as rejection; a healthy part of any relationship is "breathing," or alternating being together and being apart.

5. Ask Questions

If you're not sure what to say to a camper, just start with questions they can't simply answer with "yes" or "no." Ask them about their family, about their hobbies, about their school, about any trips they've been on. Ask them what they like about camp, what they think of the food (unless your camp food is awful – then avoid this!), what they're looking forward to doing, and so on.

6. Listen

As you converse with your campers, don't be quick to jump in and start talking about yourself and your opinions. Sometimes we are afraid of silence, so we try to fill those gaps with our own drivel, but train yourself, force yourself, to wait. Sometimes kids just need a second or two to gather their thoughts. Then, if no answer is coming, try reframing your question. Generally, though, let your campers talk to you, and show them by your attention and your posture that you care what they have to say.

7. Be Open

Don't expect your campers to open up to you if you aren't open and at least somewhat transparent with them. Choose appropriate "most embarrassing stories" to share with them to make yourself vulnerable. Laugh with them (not at them). Laugh at yourself, and don't take yourself too seriously. Let them know when you're struggling, too, but without putting it on them as if they are your therapists.

8. Give Attention

When you're with a camper, genuinely be *with* the camper. Don't be checking your watch or cell phone or responding to text messages. Don't suddenly ignore the camper when someone else comes along who is better looking or more interesting. Pay attention! Understand that many children normally never, ever get the full attention of an adult, except when they've done something wrong. Your gift of attention will often go far beyond what you expect.

9. Remember

Whenever a camper tells you something about his or her interests, commit it to memory. Personally, since my memory is about as water-tight as a fishing net, I like to write things down as soon as I'm by myself. Why do that? Because then you can review it later and bring it up to them next time you see them! "Hey, Jenna, when's your next gymnastics competition? What events are you doing?" Wow, my cabin leader remembers what I told her yesterday! She actually cares! Bingo, you have an "in" with the camper.

10. Use Touch Wisely

Positive and safe touch is something that is often lacking for many kids (others will be much too accustomed to it and may hang on your legs as you walk – literally!). When appropriate, it is often helpful to give a same-gender camper a discreet touch on the back of the shoulder or a brief side hug. It is unfortunate that this is now a "danger area," and some camps may now be telling you, "Don't do it!" In that case, you shouldn't do it, but if it is allowed, certain forms of "safe touch" can help kids know you care. "High fives" are usually safe at any camp.

11. Overcome the Fear of Rejection

One of the greatest barriers to building relationships is our fear that campers won't like us. We've been hurt before, and we don't want to be hurt again. But if we carry this attitude, we will wound those around us like we've been wounded, and the only way to end that cycle is to choose, firmly, to pursue relationships regardless of the personal cost. There is always a cost in building good relationships, which shouldn't be surprising, given what it cost God to bring us into a relationship with Himself.

12. Don't Look Down

When speaking to a camper, you may have to adjust your *altitude* (as well as your *attitude*, at times!). Physically, get down to the level of the camper you are speaking to by crouching or sitting. It's less intimidating, and it shows you care. Emotionally, don't look down on campers, either. They may be small, but they are incredibly precious in God's eyes.

13. Participate

When you get involved alongside campers, you develop shared experiences that form a bond. Play the evening games with your campers. Run with them, join in with them, be involved in their activities whenever the schedule allows. Then, when the day is winding down, and campers are talking about what they did, you are part of that conversation, maybe as a hero, maybe as a fellow-sufferer, and maybe as a failure (!), but you were there, and you were part of it. Never underestimate the power of shared experiences.

14. Express Appreciation

You can probably appreciate the fact that almost everyone appreciates being appreciated. I'm not talking about flattery or telling people how great they are when in fact they stink at something, but giving genuine, timely, kind comments when someone does something well. Think about how that makes you feel, and it will help you show appreciation to others.

15. Display Compassion

Not all of us are naturals at understanding and feeling what others are going through, so we often have to work at this by choosing to see past their behavior and by asking ourselves what the cause of this could be. This takes time and patience, as well as gentle probing at times. So many of these campers come from very tough situations, and it's our job never to assume the worst, but to feel deeply with them what they are going through. Compassion literally means to "suffer alongside" another person. Practice being empathetic.

16. Avoid Advice

When most people want advice, they ask for it, so be careful not to offer it where it isn't wanted. Saying too much at the wrong time can be seen as nagging. If you feel that advice is necessary and may be accepted, simply ask the camper, "Would you like some advice?" This allows them to ask for time or space before having to listen to your opinion. It is also helpful, if you think advice is necessary, to suggest something to the whole group rather than singling anyone out for your nuggets of wisdom.

17. Choose to Trust

Relationships are built on trust, so it is vital to be trustworthy and to choose to trust others until they prove to be untrustworthy. Follow through on what you say you will do, and be where you say you will be at the time you say you'll be there. Give campers the benefit of the doubt whenever possible. Your trust will often help them become more trustworthy, too. Sometimes we just need someone to believe in us!

18. Never Give Up!

Relationships take time, and they usually have ups and downs, even during a short camp experience. We all go through times when we're a little less loveable, so try to be patient and see campers for who they are: loved creations of the Lord God. In the same way, God never gives up on us, so we need to continue to pursue relationships and love campers for who they are, not for what they do.

Sometimes I think we get a little caught up in methodologies and forget that it isn't all that complicated to build relationships. It's not about planning special events or "quality" time because those times often don't come as you hope. Relationships come from the *quantity* of time invested, plain and simple. How many kids grow up just wishing their parents would spend time with them, just them?

Campers spell love: T-I-M-E. Be there for people, and then whatever they are going through, they'll know you care, and they will desire to be with you, too.

Discussion Questions

1. Think of a good friend you have or have had. How did you get to be good friends? What did it take on your part? On their part?

2. Why is the relationship between the cabin leader and the camper so important? Is there a more important relationship at camp?

3. There's an old saying: "People don't care what you know until they know that you care." Is that true? How does that speak to the role and task of the cabin leader?

4. Look back over the story from this chapter. What were some things Jon did that helped kids relate to him (never mind what he was thinking)?

5. Why do you think Madison was so nervous about her first time being a cabin leader? What was she most afraid of? Can you relate to that feeling? What can you do with that?

6. Does it bother you that people like Jon are so popular, despite their arrogance and insecurities? How can you act differently?

7. Of the above suggestions for building relationships, are there any that you think are of vital importance? Are there any that you have a hard time with?

CHAPTER 5

My Bed is Wet!
Understanding Campers' Needs

A LARGE CROWD of campers gathered by the lake. A thick fog lay on the lake and around the campers, and Madison was having a hard time figuring out what they were doing or why they were there at all. They all seemed to be pressed together, rocking back and forth, and slowly edging into the lake, fully clothed. Someone was insisting that they shouldn't do that – was it the lifeguard? It was so confusing. Why were the campers going down into the lake? Should she try to stop them? But she felt too slow, like she was trying to walk through wet concrete. Someone had to stop them before they all drowned! She felt panic start to set in, but she couldn't even yell.

Someone was pulling on her shoulder, and she didn't know why. *Oh, I must be dreaming*, she thought, and she rolled over.

It had been another long, tiring day, and Madison was so glad when she finally got the campers to stop whispering and go to sleep. She desperately needed eight hours of sleep, but she was grateful for the seven hours she would hopefully get before her alarm went off at 6:30.

Now her head was full of thoughts about what had happened yesterday and what she would be doing today, but with a quick prayer, a conscious effort to put those thoughts aside for now, and a soft pillow, she began to drift again into a restless sleep. Dream after dream seemed to arise and then fade away like a mist.

Entering one of those dreams, she could hear one of the campers calling her in a whisper. "Maddy! Maddy!" Again, she turned over, trying to get out of this endless cycle of dreams. Now she felt something grabbing her shoulder again, and this time it was giving her a little shake. "Maddy! Wake up!"

Okay, that was *definitely* a camper, in real life. She slowly opened her eyes and could barely see a shape hovering over her.

"Maddy! My bed is all wet!"

As Madison tried to clear the grogginess from her head, her first response was less than helpful to little Indiana. "Is it raining?" she asked.

"No! It's my sleeping bag. I *wet* it..."

"You, what? Oh..." *Okay, what do I do when this happens again?* "Okay, well, let's go deal with that. Do you have something to change into?"

"Yeah, my mom packed extra PJs."

Good job, Mom. She pulled herself up to a sitting position, willing her brain to start functioning again. "Okay, let's get you to the washroom and get you cleaned up. Grab your clothes, and I'll take your sleeping bag out and find another one for you. Oh, and give me your wet PJs, too. And go to the toilet if you need to." *Good thing the camp keeps extra sleeping bags around.*

Fifteen minutes later, Indiana was back in bed, sleeping soundly once again. Madison lay in her bed again, longing for that elusive sleep, her heart still beating a little too fast after being woken up. *Why am I doing this, again? Oh, look, just three hours until my alarm goes off. Lord, what am I doing here?!*

Jon looked at Jonesy with a grim expression. "What do you mean you *can't*? Just *do* it."

"I have a doctor's note. Nothing too strenuous."

"You were playing football yesterday!" *Little faker.*

"Yeah, but I didn't have to climb. Climbing is strenuous, so I can't do it."

Collin piped up in his high soprano from the top of the wall, "Come on, Jonesy! Let's go!"

But Jonesy wouldn't budge. There were only him and David left, and time was running out. Either the whole team completed the challenge, or they had to take a time penalty of five minutes before moving on to the next obstacle.

It had been one of those days for Jon. At breakfast, Collin kept annoying everyone with that stupid sound he could make through his nose. Well, for that he got to clean the table.

Jonesy, now *there* was a case for some budding psychiatrist. Every time they did something he didn't like, he would find an excuse not to do it and then argue with Jon until Jon gave in. Smart kid, but incredibly annoying.

Oh, and then there was Ethan, always getting mad, and usually at Collin. Not that Ethan could be *completely* blamed for that. Collin was such a little brat.

And Chris. Always doing something sneaky. Like yesterday when he thought Jon wasn't looking and pushed his sandwich off the side of the table and over the balcony. *Kid! If you don't like your sandwich, just let me know, and we'll find you something else!*

This was the third year for Jon as a cabin leader, and he still couldn't figure out how to stop his boys' constant misbehaving. It was so annoying. He looked at the girl cabins and saw them playing happily and having fun, and in the meantime, World War III broke out every time he looked away for a minute.

Sure, he knew the theory behind misbehavior and all that. People (*I guess kids are people*) have basic needs, and when they aren't met, they act out. Apparently, someone named Maslow had figured this out, as he had learned back in first-year psychology.

Yeah, well I bet Maslow didn't have little terrors in his cabin who just acted out because they wanted to wreck his day. So, they need food, drink, and rest. I give them that. Safety and security? Yup. Love and belonging... Sure, look at me loving the little brats. What more do they need, really?

He looked at his watch. "Okay, we'll have to take the penalty and make up for it at the next obstacle."

Groans emanated from the boys, and several gave nasty glances toward Jonesy. Jon thought he heard a couple of muted swear words.

"I just don't want to get sick again." Jonesy shrugged and moved away from the wall.

"You big wimp!" David called him out. "If you wanted to you *would*, but I think you're a chicken! Bawk! Bawk!" He made wing motions as strutted around, mocking Jonesy, who looked at him disdainfully.

Jon intervened once more, "No name-calling, you guys. It's no big deal. Let's spend the next few minutes strategizing about how we're going to do the spider's web. Jonesy, can you at least *crawl* through one of the bigger holes near the bottom?"

"Sure. No problem. Easy-peasy." He said it like he couldn't believe anyone would question his ability to do something so simple. Jon noticed an abundance of eye-rolls from the boys around him.

Gotta love working with young boys. That's what I give up my summers for...

Debriefing

WHEN CHILDREN COME to camp, they have a wide variety of needs and backgrounds, and it is impossible, apart from slowly building a relationship with them, to understand why they act out and what you can do about it.

However, there are some basic principles to understand and some basic needs every camper needs to have met for them to function healthily. Let's look at needs from five distinct perspectives: physical, social, emotional, spiritual, and by age.

1. Physical Needs

When we don't look after ourselves physically, it affects all aspects of our being. If your campers are not getting enough to eat or drink, they will lack energy and enthusiasm, and they may get sick or act out in unexpected ways. If they are unsafe (or feeling unsafe), nothing else will matter to them until they feel safe. And if campers don't get enough sleep, you will invite a host of problems.

Therefore, as a camp cabin leader, one of your primary duties is to ensure that each one of your charges is eating well, drinking enough, getting enough sleep, and feeling safe. You are the surrogate parent, and the primary responsibility lies with you. If your camp uses a buffet system for meals, be there in line with your kids, encouraging them to take reasonable portions and to try new things or things they may be skipping. Make sure they are taking from each of the food groups (if they can), and be aware of any allergies or intolerances they might have and where they should go to get food that is safe for them. Our kitchens need always to ensure the kids have healthy and tasty options available.

At meal times and activities, especially when it is hot, be the one to remind them to drink lots of water. As a general guideline, have them drink *more* than they feel like drinking and drink *before* they get seriously thirsty. This will cut down on heat exhaustion and other illnesses they could face if they are dehydrated. Camps need to ensure there are adequate water stations wherever the campers are active (and adequate toilet facilities nearby so that the campers aren't afraid to drink lots).

Make sure campers wear sunscreen and a hat, especially when it is hot, but be aware that kids can burn even with cloud cover in the late spring or summer. This is even more dangerous if they are near the water (or near the snow in the winter), or if they are fair-skinned. As a parent, I expect there will be some responsible adult reminding my kids to use sunscreen and making time for them to do so. I have seen parents very irate when this isn't done. Skin cancer is a very serious danger, and we want to ensure we are doing everything we can to protect our campers against it. It is *never* our job to encourage "tanning."

Other forms of protection and safety are also of vital importance. If you feel like an activity or anything the camp is doing or allowing is dangerous to your campers, it is your responsibility to speak up and let someone know — someone who can either do something about it or talk to another staff person about it. Be aware that some activities appear dangerous but are quite safe when done properly (such as rock climbing), and your camp should follow certain mandated safety standards that everyone running those activities is well-trained in.

Finally, one of the big mistakes a lot of cabin leaders and camps make is not to ensure their campers are getting enough rest. In a new environment, in a hot and sometimes noisy cabin, many kids will not sleep well, so every effort should be made to give their bodies enough time to rest and recover from the activities of the day. I have seen many camps that seem to run on the philosophy that it is their goal to tire campers out and send them home exhausted. In my experience, however, tired campers are much more likely to act out, have a hard time controlling their emotions, and enjoy camp less. If you want to cut down on behavioral problems, make sure kids get enough sleep. And be sure to tell your supervisor if your kids are exhausted so that someone can consider adjusting the schedule to an earlier bedtime.

2. Social Needs

Hopefully, by now, you are seeing that campers, and all people, need social connections. They need to feel they are an important part of a community. They need to know they are wanted and needed and loved for who they are, not just what they do.

The cabin leader's role is tricky because there is a tough balance between being a "friend" to a camper while still maintaining the respect and authority needed to lead the campers. New cabin leaders, especially, tend to either lean heavily toward trying to be a friend, or they lean too heavily toward being an authority figure. A balance between these is necessary.

Be friendly while retaining the authority needed to be in charge. Assume a relaxed, kind, and confident authority. Be an adult friend, not a peer friend. You want the campers to be friends with each other, so don't try to be the center of their universes. If you can help develop true community within the cabin, the campers will learn to rely on one another for their social connections instead of relying on just the cabin leader.

Of course, depending on the age of the campers, this will play out differently. Typically, young campers will tend to need more of a parent figure, and teenage campers will more likely want to see the cabin leader as an older, more experienced brother or sister (if they don't ignore the cabin leader completely!).

But how do we develop community in a cabin? A lot of it has to do with getting campers involved together for a bigger purpose, whether that is competing with other cabins in a game, going out on an adventure together, or trying to keep the cabin clean for cabin clean-up points.

The main thing for the cabin leader is to help everyone *contribute*. When campers have a common purpose, and when each person is using some skill or helping out in one way or another, that is when community begins to form, and each camper feels important to the whole.

If cabin leaders are enthusiastic about the cabin group they have and the fun they are going to have together at camp, half the battle has been won because those campers will want to please the cabin leader and they will not want to let one another down. Community is found best in shared experiences where everyone is contributing toward common goals.

3. Emotional Needs

What is the greatest emotional need everyone has? I think most of us would say "love." Unfortunately, "love" can be a rather nebulous concept to most people, especially these days when love, infatuation, and sex are lumped together so readily.

In God's Word, love is displayed as sacrificial, as an act of putting someone else's needs and well-being ahead of our own. That's the role of a cabin leader in a nutshell.

Some cabin leaders will complain, "How am I supposed to love my kids when I don't even like them?!"

While it is unavoidable that there will be some campers to whom we initially feel very little fondness (okay, we may rather dislike them at first), it is our responsibility, not just as cabin leaders, but as followers of Jesus, to choose to love them anyway. That is the essence of all Christian ministry, in fact, all the life of a Christian: to choose to love others, no matter who they are or how they act. This is, of course, what Jesus did for us (see Romans 5:6-8, for example).

Where does this kind of love come from? Quite simply, it is from the overflow of the love relationship we have with Jesus. We love Him because He first loved us (1 John 4:19), and we are commanded to love others (John 13:34) with that same love we received from Christ.

But what does that look like? It looks like choosing to put the needs of campers before our own, sacrificing our desires on the altar of caring for those crazy campers. Again, "People don't care what you know until they know that you care." If campers are confident they are cared for, their hearts will be opened to a relationship with you and with what you want to tell them about Jesus.

Two other words that help describe the emotional needs of a camper are "belonging" and "respect." Campers want to know they are accepted by you and by the other campers. This goes back to creating an atmosphere of community, where their voice is heard and where their gifts and abilities are used. This is also why it is so important to be present with your campers so that campers do not begin to bully or ignore other campers.

4. Spiritual Needs

I have left this until fourth, not because it is less important than the others, but because I have seen some cabin leaders *start* with this (and end with this) to the detriment of the other needs of their campers. The fact is, if you ignore your campers' basic physical, social, and emotional needs, they will usually not be interested in hearing what you have to say about God's love and plan for their lives.

Of course, equally dangerous is to build relationships and just hope that somehow people will ask about the difference Jesus has made in our lives. The good news about Jesus must be proclaimed (e.g., Rom. 10:14), and its proclamation must be accompanied by care for the needs of those around us.

I believe that all people have a massive need in their lives for purpose and meaning, and it is an amazing privilege to help campers see that they can find these needs met in Jesus Christ. We will be looking at this area much more closely in chapters 12 and 13, but for now, it is important for us to remember that much of how we deal with campers has to do with identifying their needs and proactively finding ways to help those needs be met. As we will see in the next chapter, when those needs are ignored, campers often act out in ways that are destructive to themselves and to the people around them.

5. Needs by Age

There are undoubtedly many good studies and charts to discover specific needs for different age groups. However, in teaching camp leadership over the years, I find that the details of those studies are hard to remember unless you spend many, many hours learning them. It is helpful to know a few generalities, although even this will vary at times by maturity, background, and even birth-order and age of siblings.

Still, it is helpful to know that the younger the campers are, the more they will generally rely on you to meet their physical needs. You will need to remind them to put clean clothes on, to shower, to put sunscreen on, to wear the hat their mother packed them, and so on. They will often see you as a "surrogate parent," so they will need you to be appropriately affectionate, and in return, they will often want to please you. Even the youngest at camp will have a large capacity for spiritual truth, though you will need to use concrete terms to explain it to them (abstract language will often be taken literally).

As the campers get older, they will tend to be more capable of looking after their own physical needs, and the cabin leader will become less the center of their universe. The focus will move more toward their peer group and peer acceptance. Often, they will push for their "rights" without seeing the corresponding responsibilities. Many will become interested in the opposite sex, yet they will often lack the capacity to talk about them or relate to them with any sense of propriety. They will need guidance and boundaries for all of these things.

Finally, as they get to the mid- and late-teenage years, the cabin leader becomes less and less an authority or parental figure to them, and they may be so absorbed in their fixation on their peer group that they hardly notice the cabin leader at all outside of the cabin. These campers will often go through "faith crises," where they begin to question everything they previously thought they believed. On the one hand, they want to "find themselves" and "be themselves," but that often means imitating someone that acts the way they want to be seen acting. This can be a fantastic opportunity for the cabin leader to become a key role model for those campers.

We all have needs, and campers are no different. A good cabin leader will very deliberately look to meet those needs and ensure that each camper is being looked after and thriving in the camp setting. These are the basic responsibilities of anyone who is put in charge of a group of children.

Discussion Questions

1. What are campers' most basic physical needs?

2. How do you act when your needs aren't being met?

3. What behaviors would you expect from a camper whose social needs are not being met? How can you help meet those needs?

4. What is the difference between "liking" and "loving" your campers? How can we love campers we don't particularly "like"?

5. Which needs are the most difficult to meet as a camp cabin leader: physical, social, emotional, or spiritual needs? Why?

6. What age of campers do you think you would most like to work with? What age would be hardest for you to work with? What would you have to do to be a good cabin leader to that age of campers?

CHAPTER 6

Payback Time
Discipline & Discipling

*A*shley *is definitely my type,* Jon thought as he walked back toward his cabin. *I wonder what she's doing on the weekend? Forget the weekend; I should try to see her after campfire tonight. Ah! My cabin, what do I do with the kids? Leave them for a while again?*

As he approached the cabin, Jon heard a loud thump against one of the walls, laughter, and then an angry cry. More loud thumps and sounds of shuffling feet came through the open cabin door, and as Jon turned the corner, what he saw was so chaotic it took him a moment to figure out what was going on. Clothes were scattered around on the floor, and the kids were all over the place, some yelling, some laughing, and dust was thick in the air. *Pillow fight.*

Jon could see one kid on the floor, and Kevin was above him swinging his pillow back and forth as hard as he could, and a high-pitched squeal came from his victim. *Collin – only Collin screams like that.* Someone was under the bunk, trying to hide from the other kids. *Jonesy. Big wimp.* He could also see David and Rob working together to take down little Fred, who was defiantly covering his head and trying to butt the two bigger boys who were laughing and thwacking him.

It seemed a shame to end the fun, but now that Jon was there, he had to settle them all down before Charlotte came by and got mad at them. "*No* pillow fights" she would say, those beautiful eyes flashing daggers at him. *What a stupid rule.*

Just then, Collin gave out a bigger scream than usual, jumping up with his fists swinging, catching Kevin in a sensitive area. "You little jerk!" Kevin snarled, and swung his hand at Collin's head, toppling him over once again. As Collin got up again, tears streaming from his eyes, ready to take on his much bigger adversary, Jon stepped up next to them and called out, "Woah! Woah! Take it easy guys."

Collin was too angry to be easily dissuaded, and he tried to hit Kevin again, but Jon quickly stepped in between them and grabbed Collin's arms. "Enough!" he yelled. "Everyone, back to your bunks! *NOW!*"

Collin was too angry to settle down, his face beet-red and streaked with tears. "I'm gonna kill him! I'm gonna kill him! I hate this place! Stupid camp." He then started to use some words that shouldn't be repeated, and Jon began to get angry.

"Enough, Collin! *Get* to your bunk! *Now!*" Collin suddenly seemed to hear him for the first time. He jerked his arms out of Jon's grasp and sullenly went back to his bunk.

"Okay, who started all this?" There was silence for the first time since Jon had come in.

Jon took a deep breath. "Look, you guys know you're not supposed to have pillow fights, right?"

David piped up, "You let us yesterday."

"That's not the point. I was here, so it was okay."

Jonesy, who had by now found his way out from under the bed, rolled on his bunk to face Jon. "Pillow fights aren't allowed at camp. So, we shouldn't have them *anytime.*"

Jon replied, "Well, exactly. Not if you guys can't handle them. Come on guys; you're going to get me in trouble if you act like this. I can let you get away with some things, but if you make that much noise, someone's going to get real mad at us." *And I'll look like I can't handle my own cabin.*

"That's stupid. If we're not allowed to have pillow fights, we shouldn't have them."

"Okay, Jonesy," Jon said in a very patronizing voice, "just because *you're* afraid to get hurt, doesn't mean everyone else has to suffer."

Jonesy gave him a withering look. "I'm not *afraid.* It's just *dumb.*"

"You're dumb," said Rob, with a laugh. Jonesy didn't take the bait and ignored him.

Jon was getting a headache. "Okay, listen. No more pillow fights unless I'm here and say it's okay. Kevin, no more picking on Collin. Collin, no more *freaking* out. Any more of this and all you guys will have to miss the game tonight. Seriously. Are we good?"

Jonesy wouldn't let it go. "Why should I be punished when I didn't do anything?"

Collin was still upset, though his face was a little less red than it was earlier. His high-pitched voice grated on Jon. "Yeah! I was just trying to read my book, and David and Rob got up and started bugging me, and then Kevin called me a 'retard,' just because I didn't want to get up and have a pillow fight. You said we had to stay in our bunks, so why don't you punish the guys who disobeyed you?"

"I didn't say anyone was going to miss the game tonight. Just if this happens again. Gee, you guys, just shut up for a while, will you? You're acting like 4-year-olds!"

"*I* didn't do anything." By now, Jonesy was really starting to get to Jon.

"Be *quiet*, Jonesy. You don't have to comment on everything I say. You can clean the table at supper."

"I did it at lunch today. *That's* not fair."

"Then stop *talking*! Man, you guys are ridiculous!"

"Everything okay, Jon? Do you need a hand with anything?"

The voice behind him at the door surprised him, and he turned to see Charlotte standing there, hands on her hips, with an unhappy look on her face and an eyebrow arched. *Wow, beautiful. Almost worth the trouble...*

"No, I think we just got it sorted out. A little discipline problem, but we're okay now."

"You guys weren't pillow fighting, were you? I heard some complaints that there was a lot of noise coming from your cabin. *Siesta* is supposed to be a quiet, restful time, right?"

"Yeah, I just stepped out for a second and came back, and they were doing that. You know boys!"

Charlotte looked like she was about to say something and then held it back. There was a brief silence, and then she looked around the room at the boys and then at the mess on the floor. "You guys better get this cleaned up now. Next activity is in 10 minutes." She turned and left without a further glance at their hapless cabin leader.

Jon rolled his eyes. "Thanks, guys. Thanks for getting *me* in trouble. Okay, you heard her, let's get this place cleaned up. And Collin, go wash your face. Well done, guys, *well done.*"

"Charlotte, you got a minute?"

Charlotte swiveled in her chair to see Madison standing at the open door to the program office. "Hey, Maddy! Sure, what can I do for you?"

"Well, I don't want to take too much time, but I have some questions about how to deal with a situation with a couple of my kids."

"You want to go for a walk? Is this an off-block for you?"

"Yes, it is. That would be great." *Hmm, Charlotte's more approachable than I thought.*

"So, what's going on?" They walked down the road toward the pond and the nature trail.

"I think one of my girls is getting bullied by the other girls, and I'm not sure what to do about it. She's been crying a lot, and at first, I thought, well, she's probably homesick. So I tried to get her more involved in things and really looked out for her. When I asked her what was wrong, she wouldn't say."

"That could be homesickness. It's sometimes hard to tell." Ducks on the pond suddenly flew off, squawking at them for the interruption.

"Yeah, that's what I thought. But then today, when I came out of the bathroom, Kayla, that's the girl, was in tears again, and some of the other girls were laughing, right until they saw me walk in, and then they were quiet all of a sudden. Of course, they all denied anything was going on when I asked, but from the look on Kayla's face, she really wanted to say something."

"Hmm, that doesn't sound good."

"No. So later on, when the kids were heading to their activities, I asked Kayla to stay behind for a minute, and I asked her if she was doing okay. She said she was fine, so I got a little more direct and asked her if she was getting along with the other girls okay. She hesitated a bit and then said she didn't think Brooke liked her very much. I tried to find out what she meant, but she didn't want to say anything else, and she went to her activity."

"Hmm, sounds like there's something going on there. What do you know about Brooke?" A frog "gleeped" and jumped into the pond.

"That's the thing. She's a bit of a ring-leader in the cabin. The other girls look to her as a leader, and they all seem to want to please her. Not that Brooke's even all that nice to them, but she seems to have a bit of control over them. Actually, she can be down-right rude to the other girls sometimes, but they still seem to follow her. And it looks to me like Kayla's on the outside looking in, some of the time."

Charlotte stopped and thought for a moment. "Does Kayla have any other friends in the cabin?"

"Not really. Well, maybe Allison, but she's fairly quiet and keeps mostly to herself. She's sweet and a people-pleaser."

"I think you're probably right, Maddy. Sounds like Brooke is a bit of a bully, and Kayla may be on the bad end of that. What do you think you should do?"

Madison frowned. "I'm not sure. I guess I need to take Brooke aside and talk to her. Maybe if I get to know her a little better, and her situation, I can encourage her to include Kayla in things a bit more."

"Yes, exactly. If Brooke is being a bully, it needs to stop. As you know, we have a 'no tolerance' policy for bullying. But we also need to recognize that if she is acting out that way, there are reasons for her behavior as well. Not that those reasons *excuse* her behavior, but they do provide context for how we can help her become better socially and more kind. There's a good chance that she gets bullied at her school or in her home, and this is an opportunity for her to have more power and not feel so helpless."

"Okay, thanks, Charlotte. I really love these girls, and I want them to have a great time. And ultimately, I want them to know that God loves them and sent Jesus to die to set them free!"

Charlotte smiled and gave Madison a quick side-hug. "Atta girl! You seem to be figuring out this cabin leader role just fine. I knew you would."

"Well, it's even harder than I thought, in some ways, but so great, too. My girls are so precious!"

"And that's why you always need to remember why we're here. Especially when the kids mess up. The point isn't simply to make them obey, but to encourage them to grow and develop."

"Yeah, I remember at staff training you said the goal was 'discipleship' not just 'discipline' in dealing with bad behavior. I've been thinking about that a lot, whenever the girls do something they shouldn't. How can I turn this into something that draws them closer to God instead of just trying to make them behave or instead of just trying to punish them? But to be honest, sometimes I just want to punish them!"

Charlotte chuckled and nodded knowingly. "They can certainly make you feel that way at times. But if you truly love them, you'll want what's best for them in the long run, not just what solves the immediate issue. Make *disciples*, Maddy!"

"Thanks again for your time and helping me think this through. I'm going to go show Brooke and Kayla how much I care for them, and help them know God's love. Please pray for me? And them?"

Charlotte put her arm around Madison's shoulders again and closed her eyes. "Let's do that right now, hey?"

Debriefing

MOST NEW CABIN LEADERS (and many experienced cabin leaders) struggle when they have to deal with campers misbehaving. Of course, every parent struggles with this, too, so it's no surprise.

The temptation is always to take the easiest way out, which is usually the worst choice in the long-run. Two common shortcuts can be called "punishing" and "ignoring."

Punishing

When kids act up, some adults immediately try to figure out who is at fault (often incorrectly), blame that child, and quickly choose a punishment. Billy goofs off at supper and spills his milk? Simple solution, Billy goes to his room and doesn't get dessert. Suzy comes home late from a party? Fine, she's grounded for a month. Jonesy talks back to Jon? He cleans the table for the next meal.

Punishment "works" on one level. The situation is dealt with quickly, and the authority figure doesn't have to deal with it anymore, at least in the short-term. Sure, the child might be angry or sad, but they have learned a valuable lesson and hopefully won't act out that way again. It works in the army – obey or be punished. So why not with kids?

The problem is the lack of love and support experienced by the child and offered by the adult. It leads to resentment and anger that will eventually find its way out, often in later rebellion. Or worse, they become afraid to try anything new for fear of punishment. Children struggle to do the right thing, and they want to be understood, not simply punished. They want to know that the authority figure cares for them. There may be times when some form of punishment is needed, but when it is given indiscriminately, out of convenience instead of out of loving support, it is very dangerous.

Ignoring

As dangerous as it is to use punishment as a shortcut, ignoring bad behavior and hoping it will go away may be even worse. Some parents (and some camp cabin leaders) are so lenient that children grow up knowing no boundaries. They desperately wish someone would just tell them "No! Don't do it!" Children with boundaries will often push them or cross them, but they are glad they are there.

I heard about an elementary school that removed their fences to help the children feel more "free" and less "constricted." They were surprised by the results. With fences, most kids felt free to play throughout the entire property, right up to the fences. The fences gave them security because they knew how far they could go. Sometimes kids would sneak over or through the fences, but at least they knew when they were off the property and when they were breaking the rules. However, when the fences were removed, the children tended to stay in the middle of the property, away from the edges. They felt less safe. Instead of bringing freedom, it brought uncertainty.

We need fences in our lives. When we know the boundaries we are supposed to live within, we feel safe right up to those boundaries, and we know when we've gone beyond them. But without boundaries, freedom disappears.

Jon exemplified both tendencies of punishing and ignoring. At first, when he sees the campers misbehaving, he tries to make everyone happy again without dealing with what had happened. But when they didn't cooperate, he yelled at them. Then he threatened them with missing the evening game. Eventually, he picked on the one kid who hadn't done anything wrong (Jonesy) and wanted to punish him for questioning his decision on the matter.

Jon is great with kids when they are out playing football, and everything is okay. He often shows grace and maturity, at least on the surface. He knows how to play a crowd and how to engage kids. But this time, maybe because he's tired, or because he knows he messed up by not being there and by letting things get out of hand, he tries both shortcuts to avoid dealing with the misbehavior.

In fact, unlike Madison, who is paying attention to some subtle signs that there is bullying going on in her cabin, Jon ignores the blatant bullying that occurs right in front of his eyes. He is trying to be fun and easy-going with his campers, but in the long-run, he is doing no favor for those children. They will leave camp having been failed by yet another adult who could have truly built into them. His inconsistent boundaries are harming them, not helping them.

Discipling

The purpose of "camper discipline" is to motivate campers to do what is right and constructive. It involves teaching and modeling behaviors that will help them develop positive habits and relationships. As a camp cabin leader, your goal is not to make things easier for yourself but to love the campers and to build into them. Think of it as "discipling" – making followers of Jesus.

It is helpful to think about how God deals with our shortcomings when we're His children, as seen in the following passages.

> The Lord is compassionate and merciful, slow to get angry and filled with unfailing love. He will not constantly accuse us, nor remain angry forever. He does not punish us for all our sins; he does not deal harshly with us, as we deserve. For his unfailing love toward those who fear him is as great as the height of the heavens above the earth. He has removed our sins as far from us as the east is from the west. The Lord is like a father to his

children, tender and compassionate to those who fear him. For
he knows how weak we are; he remembers we are only dust.

~Psalm 103:8-14

As you endure this divine discipline, remember that God is
treating you as his own children... For our earthly fathers
disciplined us for a few years, doing the best they knew how. But
God's discipline is always good for us so that we might share in
his holiness. No discipline is enjoyable while it is happening—it's
painful! But afterward there will be a peaceful harvest of right
living for those who are trained in this way.

~Hebrews 12:7a, 10-11

My child, don't reject the Lord's discipline, and don't be upset
when he corrects you. For the Lord corrects those he loves, just
as a father corrects a child in whom he delights.

~Proverbs 3:11-12

Seven Golden Principles of a "Discipling" Discipline

These verses remind us of the following principles for a discipling
form of discipline.

1. Our ability to provide good discipline has a lot to do with our character.

Like our Heavenly Father, we need to be gracious, compassionate,
slow to anger, and abounding in love. Unlike God, we have a hard time
with that! But *who we are* will determine our ability to seek the best for
these campers. One of the areas we must deal with to be effective with
kids is any problem of anger we have. If you struggle in that area,
prayerfully submit that to God, and never yell angrily at campers or
start losing control. Get help and accountability if that is an issue for
you, and if you feel yourself "losing it," leave immediately (if possible)
and get help with your campers.

2. Discipline is not the same as giving the punishment one deserves.

Sometimes campers feel like adults are out to get them, and to be
honest, I've heard cabin leaders and parents talk as if what they are

really looking for is *revenge!* Despite our many sins, God does not always accuse, nor does He stay angry at us, nor does He give us what we deserve. Instead, He offers mercy, grace, and forgiveness. This doesn't mean you can't find creative ways for campers to learn from their mistakes (such as cleaning the cabin if they made the mess), but any consequences should be connected to what they did wrong, and they should be given with an attitude of reconciliation, not to be punitive.

3. Our love must be sacrificial – like God's.

God removed our transgressions by dying on a cross. Instead of just saying, "Well, if that's the way they're going to be, then to hell with them," He showed His compassion by paying the price for our sins that we deserved to pay. So when it comes to discipline, we need to ask ourselves, what am I willing to do to help them with this sin problem they have?

When our son was a toddler, he disobeyed us and intentionally spilled a whole ice cream bucket of fresh blackberries down our carpeted stairway, staining each and every stair in several places. I knew he was incapable of cleaning them up, yet I knew it needed to be done, so I tried to think of how I could teach him the cost of his disobedience. I had him sit at the top of the stairs and watch me while I scrubbed and cleaned for the next hour or longer. I was angry, and I wanted to punish him, but something told me that this would help him understand the consequences of his actions. Had he been a little older, I would have had him do the cleaning, yet in my love for him, I would have still been there, beside him, scrubbing away.

Romans 5:8 says, "But God showed his great love for us by sending Christ to die for us while we were still sinners." Other translations say that Jesus died for us while we were still "helpless" or "powerless." In God's love for us, in His compassion, He did for us what we couldn't do.

4. Always consider human frailty.

Be very careful to distinguish between *mistakes* and *misbehavior.* This is important from a spiritual perspective as well. God doesn't call us out for honest mistakes we make, like accidentally backing into a garbage can, forgetting to pay a bill, or accidentally hurting someone's feelings due to a misunderstanding. These things happen. Granted, they can also be because of carelessness, which can be sinful, but a lot of the time, we just have a lot on our mind, and we do things we regret later that aren't issues of rebellion.

Expect campers to mess up. We encourage them to come to camp, out of their comfort zones, and then we tend to expect them to do everything perfectly. Well, they *will* make mistakes. They'll forget things you feel like you told them 17 times. They'll struggle to get along with a bunch of kids they have never met before, much less lived with. They'll get excited and have trouble settling down. Sometimes they'll even let words slip that they don't mean to. Does that make them terrible persons?

Just remember, they're kids, and even *you* mess up from time to time, so why not relax a bit? You need to choose your battles carefully and not harp on everything they don't do perfectly. Don't assume a motivation for an action when you often don't even know your own motivations for the things you do. Gently remind them when they forget things, even when you've already reminded them. Be patient and long-suffering.

5. Treat campers as if they were your own children.

If your campers know you love them, most discipline problems are relatively easy to deal with. If you build a solid relationship with them, they will want to please you. And if you treat them respectfully, they will usually respect your efforts to discipline them.

One thing that helps greatly with this is to make your *expectations* clear up front. I used to have just one "rule" in my cabins: *Respect*. Respect for each other, respect for property, and respect for the camp program. So, when they were mean to each other or late for something or grabbing things that weren't theirs, I often simply had to ask them gently if that was respectful, and they would usually realize it wasn't and change what they were doing.

Some cabin leaders will ask their campers on the first day to help make a list of rules for the cabin for living together. This is a great way to gain buy-in, and campers usually want more rules than you would have given them yourself! If the kids know from the beginning how they are supposed to act, it will pay dividends down the road when they find themselves not doing those things.

Just like a loving parent, you need to have the best interests of the campers at heart, and they will generally respond well and cooperate.

6. Discipline is always for the good of the person being disciplined.

Note that God always disciplines us for His purposes and for our ultimate good. It never seems 'pleasant' at the time, but it helps mold us into the people He wants us to be. So, when we discipline, we need to make sure we are truly acting in the interests of the camper, and are not simply trying to make life easier for ourselves.

How we discipline is vital. At the end of the day, did this episode draw the campers nearer to God or farther away? Did it deepen the camper's relationship with you, or drive the camper farther away?

7. The end goal of discipline is holiness, righteousness, and peace.

What do we want in our cabins? Why do we bother with dealing with misbehavior? Hopefully, it is because we want campers to become better people, and we want our cabins to have peace and harmony, to be safe places for kids to learn and grow and relate.

God wants to transform us and make us holy and righteous through a relationship with Jesus. Holiness doesn't come from trying harder or following rules. Therefore, discipline needs to encourage people *toward* God, not away from Him. And when we truly pursue God, we will find peace in other relationships as well.

Final Tips for Disciplining

Cabin leaders are often fearful of having to discipline their campers, not wanting to be too harsh, yet not allowing things to get out of control. It is easy to get caught up in the moment and react poorly. However, if we truly want the best for our campers, as God does for us, disciplining will become increasingly natural.

Here are a few final tips to help you deal with discipline issues:

- Deal with misbehavior in a timely fashion. If you ignore it, it will naturally get worse, not better. Don't let one camper ruin things for everyone else.

- Choose your battles carefully, distinguishing between mistakes and misbehavior.

- Deal with campers privately, away from others.

- Don't raise your voice in anger (make sure you're calm before trying to deal with it).

- Don't use "guilt trips."

- Don't question the spirituality of a camper (e.g., "How can you call yourself a Christian when you…?").

- Hear all sides of the story before deciding what to do.

- Ask the camper to tell you what they did wrong.

- Ask the camper what they think should be the consequences.

- Remember that consequences should always connect clearly to the wrong committed.

Discipline is never easy for the one giving or receiving it, but if it is done compassionately, with "discipling" firmly in mind, the lasting benefits far outweigh the momentary pain it causes.

Discussion Questions

1. How do "fences" or "boundaries" bring freedom? How do we let campers know where the fences are?

2. Why is it easier to 'punish' campers than it is to 'discipline' them? What is the difference? Why is discipline more effective in the long run?

3. Why is it ineffective to ignore misbehavior and hope it will go away? Think about and share a time when you saw or experienced that approach fail.

4. How much harder is it to deal with misbehavior when we are tired or stressed out? How can we be sure that we aren't the main problem? How does our character come into this?

5. Does grace mean there are no consequences? How can consequences and grace work together when dealing with camper misbehavior?

6. How can you tell the difference between mistakes and misbehavior? What are some things to consider?

7. Why is it so important for campers to know expectations up front, before they have the opportunity to misbehave?

8. What is the end goal of godly discipline? Why is it important to always keep this in mind?

BECOMING A BETTER LEADER

CHAPTER 7

Dropping Off the Edge of a Cliff
Leading Activities

O KAY, IS THERE ANYTHING ELSE we should know when we're doing the low ropes course?" Maddy looked around at the campers, but very few were even paying attention. Donny had his finger in his ear, digging for treasures, and little Charlie was watching the clouds. Phil was playing with a small stick. Dylan was swaying back and forth like he had to go to the bathroom. Most of the rest were looking at the course or making faces at each other.

Bryan raised his hand and began talking before it was acknowledged. "We need spotters."

Maddy smiled. "Well, good idea, but no, not really. If you want a spotter on any of the elements, you can ask, and someone will help you. But for the most part, you should keep a couple of yards away from people on the course, especially if they are on a part that could swing and hit you. Anyone else?"

"Only one person on a thing at a time?" asked Blake.

"I already *said* that" Franky laughed, and some of the other boys tittered a bit.

"No, you didn't!" Blake protested.

"Yeah, he did!" Several boys chimed in.

"Well, *I* don't remember him saying that," Blake grunted.

Franky replied, "You were watching some *girls* go by when I said it!" All the boys laughed.

"Shut up – was not!"

"Were too. *Loser.*"

Maddy quickly tried to gain control. "Okay, guys, that's not nice or necessary. Do you guys want to get on the course or not?"

"Not really," Blake said, pouting a little bit.

"That's because you're a pumpkin-head!" Franky exclaimed. Everyone except Blake laughed. He was kicking at a pebble.

"Enough!" Maddy was getting so frustrated by these boys. *Why on earth do I have to deal with these brats?* She'd already had this group at archery yesterday. Jackie, who was her assistant for the activity, sighed loudly but didn't offer any help. *Okay, Jesus loves them, and so do I. And so do I. And so do I. Really, I do.*

Maddy took a deep breath. "Okay, boys, let's show some respect to each other, okay? Any more nasty comments and you're going to have to sit at the side, watching instead of participating. And then you can come with me afterward and explain to Charlotte why you are being so mean."

"Maddy? It's too hot. Do we have to do this?" moaned Charlie.

"That's a good question, Charlie. No, like we said earlier, you don't *have* to do any of the activities. Remember what we said about "challenge by choice" at the beginning of the week? You can choose what you do, but you have to stay at the activity whether you do it or not. But you'll probably have a lot more fun if you give it a try. Look, how many of you have done this before?"

Most of them raised a hand. "Okay, so is there anything important from the rules that we didn't cover? No, okay, good. I think you guys did a great job remembering what to do here. So, what we're going to do is give everyone a chance to go on any part of it, and then we'll have a friendly little competition. Any questions?"

Isaac piped up, "Do we have to start at the beginning?"

"No, you don't have to. We don't want a big line-up, so if people don't want to wait at the beginning, they can just jump in anywhere on the course that no one else is doing. Just remember, only one person on each element, and you need to do them in a counter-clockwise direction. Everyone point the right direction? Good. Okay, let's have some fun! And if anyone needs any tips, help, or a spotter, let me or Jackie know, okay?"

As Madison was talking, some of the boys were already creeping toward the start of the obstacle course, and when she finished talking, three of them practically ran over each other trying to be first. Madison looked at Jackie and said. "Could you please hang out on this end and make sure they don't kill themselves, or each other?" Jackie shrugged and walked over, saying nothing to the boys who were still shoving each other.

You could at least engage the kids, Maddy thought. She'd taught activities before with Jackie and been very unimpressed. At team building, she'd had to leave with a camper to get a Band-Aid, and when she came back, Jackie was sitting on a log, thirty feet from where the kids were attempting the "Spider's Web." *Seriously, Jackie, what are you here for?*

It had already been a long day, and Maddy was tired. This was her fifth block of Low Ropes today, and she just wanted to sit down for a while. The girls and the older boys she'd had earlier were fine, but this was a tough group to end with. *Lord, please give me the strength, perseverance, and joy to get through this hour, and help me to love these kids like You do.*

"Come on kid, you can do it!" *Seriously, stop your blubbering and come down!* Jon was fed up, and he wasn't interested in hiding it.

Breanna was twelve years old, short, and a little on the heavier side. She had no good friends at camp, but this was her fourth year there. When her mom had asked her why she liked camp so much, she had a hard time expressing what it was. "Well, it's just, well, it's fun. I mean, not all the activities, so much, but when I'm there, it's like I'm accepted for who I am. Especially by the staff. And the chapels and campfires are great. I love the songs."

Most of the activities, however, still terrified her. Team sports were brutal, and she rarely touched the ball or contributed much to her teams, but at least those didn't really depend on her. Heights were the worst, and this was the first year she had even tried the rock climbing. It wasn't going well.

"You've got this, Bree!" That was Sierra, a fellow camper. She was always so encouraging.

Breanna had somehow slowly made it up the easiest climb, but the thought of being lowered on the rope had made her panic. Then she made the mistake of looking down, and the tears started to flow. *Why do I always have to cry?!* That simply infuriated her, and she regained control long enough to decide she was safe as long as she held onto the rock.

"Okay, Breanna, lots of people waiting. Just lean back on the rope, and I'll lower you down. Trust me, we do this all the time. These ropes are rated at 5000 pounds, you know." *Come on kid, this is so annoying!*

Breanna wasn't convinced. The rational part of her knew that the ropes, carabiners, harness, and everything were safe. That wasn't the problem. Her issue was that her hands and feet weren't responding to anything her brain was trying to tell them. She was stuck.

"Shall I go up?" Tami looked at Jon and raised an eyebrow. She had just finished belaying another girl.

"I suppose you'd better," Jon sighed. This would mean kids would get fewer climbs. He didn't know why he found that so annoying, but he despised inefficiency and wasted time when he led activities.

Soon Tami had taken the path up to the top of the rock and was lowering herself on a safety rope down to Breanna. "I'm coming, Breanna!" Soon she was beside her, and she reached out and gave Breanna a little pat and rub on the back. "You're okay, Bree. I'll help you down."

Breanna's tears started to flow again. "I'm s-s-sorry, Tami! I was fine on the way up! I feel like such an idiot!"

"You're doing great! Don't worry about it! You finally had the courage to climb this year, and look at you! You made it to the top!"

"Yeah, I guess I did, didn't I?" A small smile almost crept onto Breanna's face. "But now what do I do?"

"Well, you let go of that rock and let Jon lower you down."

"That's the problem. I can't let go." Breanna looked like she had the weight of the world on her face, her concern was so great. "I know the ropes can hold me, but I can't do it."

"It's kind of like trusting in God, isn't it?" Tami asked. "I know God is strong, I know He loves me, and I know He's good, but then things come up in my life that freak me out, and I have such a hard time trusting Him."

"Yeah, I do the same thing." Breanna thought for a moment. "So, this rope is like God, and I just have to let go and trust Him?"

"Sort of like that, yeah."

"God's a lot skinnier than I was expecting. Are you sure He's going to hold me?"

Tami looked at her and winked. "You got this, girl! It would hold a truck if we needed it to."

"Okay, well, I'm going to try, then. But stay with me, okay?"

"Sure. I can even hold your hand if you want."

"I think I want both my hands on the rope. But an arm behind me might help."

"Let's do this!"

Jon called up, "We ready to rock and roll up there?"

"We're getting there," Tami replied.

"Just make sure you've got me," called Breanna, in a voice more confident than she expected.

Breanna took one hand off the rock and grabbed her rope. She knew it wasn't necessary, but it felt safer. *Now the other hand... Obey me! I will trust in the rope. It is strong. My harness is strong. God is strong. I am perfectly safe.*

She felt a little squeeze on her back from Tami and watched her own hand move off the rock and onto the rope. She gave out a small shriek as her weight settled onto the rope and she dropped a little. But it held! Then she slowly began to descend, and she even remembered to put her feet out onto the rock like they had been taught to do. Before she knew it, she saw the ground beneath her, and she let her bottom be lowered all the way to the ground before she tried to put her feet down.

"Atta girl!" exclaimed Tami.

Relief poured over Breanna. Her legs felt weak, but she was so grateful to be back on the ground. "Thanks, Tami. And thanks, Jon, for getting me down safely. Sorry I took so long."

Jon grimaced. "Well, I've never dropped anyone yet. Next time, just trust me, and it'll be a lot easier for all of us." He undid the carabiner.

"But now you know you can do it, Bree!" Tami offered. "And each time you climb from now on, it'll feel a little easier. And that's just like trusting God. Each time we face tough circumstances and put our trust in Him, we see Him come through, and then we're able to trust Him more the next time, or in bigger things."

Breanna nodded as she began to remove her harness. "Well, I'm not going to run home and go bungee jumping, if that's what you mean, but I might, and I mean *might*, try the high ropes course sometime."

Tami looked impressed. "Wow, now *that* would be something! I hope I'm there to see it!"

Debriefing

ONE OF MY GREATEST camp "pet peeves" is having great activities that are led by people who take all the fun away. I have often been frustrated by seeing activity leaders doing a poor job. Oh sure, many do absolutely fantastic work with the campers at activities, but I think this is one area at many camps I've been to that often needs more training and more accountability.

I'm not talking about unsafe behaviors. In the areas that have significant potential danger, such as horseback riding, rock climbing, waterfront, and high ropes courses, we tend to be pretty good at knowing the established standards and keeping them. I am so thankful for that!

But in my experience, it tends to be the activities with less obvious danger where our standards and instruction are often deficient. Like in leading the team-building course, a hike, the low ropes course, field sports, or crafts. Perhaps it's because many leaders and campers see these activities as "fillers" until they can go do the more exciting things.

Well! Let me tell *you* something! There should never, *ever* be a filler activity! If we have an opportunity to spend time with campers at an activity, we have the privilege and responsibility to make that hour the best it can possibly be for those campers.

Granted, it can be challenging. Campers and leaders alike are often tired and unmotivated, especially during the afternoons, and even more so on hot days. Sometimes activity leaders have not been adequately trained, a few are tired (or lazy), and many others just need more accountability and inspiration. Some campers, too, are extremely difficult to motivate or control. But there are some principles that can still make all the difference in the world.

1. Be proactive

If you are leading an activity, and you don't know what you are supposed to be doing, guess whose responsibility it is to find out? Yes, yours! As soon as you know you're on the schedule for something you aren't familiar with, go and talk to someone to let them know you need some help. Sometimes it will be assumed you know or that you've done it before, but it was an oversight. Other times, you will have someone else there who has run it before. But if you are going to be running an activity, it is also your responsibility to have the technical expertise to run it well and safely.

You should also show up to each activity *early* to ensure that everything is set up and ready to go. Sometimes, due to scheduling, this may be impossible, but as much as it relies on you, you should be there before the campers, so you are ready to go when they arrive. Part of this is for your own readiness, but it is also a form of respect to the campers that they are not kept waiting.

2. Treat each activity like it is the best one in the whole camp

When campers arrive, immediately set a tone of excitement for the activity. Even if you are a quiet and shy person, you will need to force yourself to "fake" it, until it becomes more natural. If the campers see that *you* think this is going to be an amazing time, they will usually want to participate.

3. Be aware of expectations

Some campers will come expecting the activity to be lame, and it is your job to demonstrate that it will be awesome! Also, be aware that boys and girls tend to approach activities differently. Often boys will look at an activity to be attacked and solved and experienced individually, whereas girls may be thinking more in terms of how this will be fun in a social way. Obviously, the lines are not necessarily strictly boy versus girl, but it helps to ask yourself, "What does this camper want out of this time?"

4. Make allowances for different abilities

It is also important to realize that different skill levels will affect a camper's approach to an activity. Where possible, activities should be set to allow different skill levels to enjoy the activity equally, like different difficulty routes at a climbing wall, or apparatuses at a skate park that appeal to different levels of skaters. Many team-building exercises and activities are great this way for utilizing different skills, abilities, and even body types.

Sometimes, however, you'll need to be creative, maybe by changing the rules in soccer to make it more even (such as ensuring everyone on a team has to touch the ball before a goal is scored) or by encouraging highly skilled campers to take on a handicap. Some groups may have less ability than needed for certain activities, so altering the rules may help them find success as a group.

5. Use internal motivations

It is very difficult to make someone do something they don't want to do. The objective for the leader is to present the activity in such a way that they want to do it. Rather than just *telling* them what they need to do (external motivation), try *asking* them what would be a good challenge for them, such as what they think they can accomplish (internal motivation).

If they don't think they can get everyone over the wall, ask them what a good number would be for them to attempt. Rather than assuming an activity is "one size fits all," give them the ownership of what they want to accomplish. If it turns out too hard or too easy, maybe ask them if they want to try again with different parameters. "Do you think we could do this in 30 seconds this time? Or what time would be a good challenge for us?"

6. Offer "challenge by choice"

Similarly, we never force campers to participate in an activity. We want to make it attractive to them so they will choose to participate, but campers need to be empowered to choose if and to what extent they will join in. Where possible, we need to be flexible and avoid "all or nothing" situations.

A child doesn't want to play volleyball. Okay, well instead of telling them where they must sit to be out of the way, can we include them by making them ref or scorekeeper? If they are afraid to go over the wall, can they be a spotter? Can they help retrieve or find arrows if they don't want to shoot them? Or maybe they could help coach people and look out for the five keys that you taught them of how to shoot. Motivate kids by making things fun and non-threatening, but don't try to guilt them into something they don't want to do.

7. Be sensitive to fears

It is very easy to miss all the signals campers are giving that they are truly terrified. This is especially true, I have found, with guy staff not knowing how to deal with girls. Somehow, they think that all the camper has to do is "get over it," and she'll be fine. But it's not acceptable to bully kids into doing something they are not ready to do, whether it's going down a rappel or trying a skateboard move. Yes, some kids just need a little incentive, and maybe that's the way the *leader* is, but that doesn't mean every child operates that way. Some children just aren't ready to do it, and that's fine. Be careful not to be so focused on the task that you miss the relational aspects of the activity you are leading.

8. Look for opportunities

A good camp leader is always going to keep the mission of the camp in mind, and that mission, as discussed earlier, is *transformation* – offering them experiences that draw them to Jesus, so that He can transform their lives through the gospel. And so, at activities, like everywhere at the camp, we need to be looking for what I will call "transformative opportunities," where we can speak life into them and use "teachable moments" to help them grasp truths.

Instead of just running an activity, we should be building relationships with kids and reaching out to them with the love of Christ. Get in the habit of "looking past the task to the lesson." See what it is that can be learned or experienced that will develop the campers. Sometimes it is the problem-solving or the teamwork that matters a lot more than completing some task.

9. Don't play second fiddle

It can be hard to be the "other leader" at an activity, the one who is mainly there for support, rather than the one who is in charge and leading the activity. It is easy for that person to take their role less seriously and become an observer instead of stepping up and helping. The fact is, the person in that position often has a much better opportunity to relate to the campers and encourage them and help them than the person running the activity. So take that role seriously and also actively look for opportunities to support the person in charge.

If you are the person in charge, do whatever you can to involve the other leaders. Give them significant roles and communicate with them reminders of what they need to do to support the activity and the campers. If possible, talk about roles and expectations before the campers arrive. Remember, the mission of camp ministry is also to the staff and volunteers, so help other leaders develop as well.

10. Be aware of secondary dangers

Sometimes it is easy to focus on the activity and all the safety standards and forget about other dangers, such as dehydration and sunburn. Be sure to include these things in your safety standards, and write them into your activity plans.

11. There are no boring activities, only boring leaders!

I find it very discouraging to walk by an activity and see campers and staff totally disengaged. The leaders are sitting around "supervising" while the kids half-heartedly go through the motions. It is such a crime when you get feedback from a camper or a parent that certain activities were boring. Really? Nothing at camp should ever be boring if the leaders are leading well and engaging the kids.

As much as safety and common sense allow, leaders should join in with the kids in the activities to make it a shared experience. Don't *send* them to play touch football, *join* them and be the one who is making it fun! Be a "playing coach." When everything else in the program fails (which should be very seldom), enthusiasm by the leaders always wins out.

I've taken kids out in the pouring rain with a compass and a fake set of directions I had scribbled down, tromping around the camp for an hour, supposedly looking for treasure, and had kids tell me it was the highlight of their week. Why? Because my buddy and I were enthusiastic and made it fun. While the rest of the kids were jammed inside playing some less-than-wonderful games, we were out exploring and laughing our heads off. Enthusiasm is contagious! Don't be a boring leader.

Becoming a good leader at activities is not too different from being a good cabin leader. Most of it has to do with keeping the main thing at the forefront: camp is for the campers, and so we're going to do everything we can to engage them, to love them, to make things safe, and to make things fun. Lead your activities wisely and relationally, and everyone should have a great time.

Discussion Questions

1. If you were a camper previously, what were your favorite activities? Why were they your favorite? Were there any leaders that made them fun?

2. Have you ever been at an activity that was boring because the leaders were boring? What do you wish they had done differently?

3. How can you quickly change the expectations that campers have of an activity that might seem boring to them?

4. What is the difference between "internal" and "external" motivation? Why is one often better than the other?

5. What is the idea behind "challenge by choice"? Why do you think this is important for campers to understand?

6. How can we use activities as opportunities to build into campers?

7. Do you believe the idea that "there are no boring activities, only boring leaders"? If campers are bored, is it usually the activity or the leaders to blame? What can you do about that?

CHAPTER 8

Extreme Wolfman & Confused Campers
Planning to Succeed

H EY, JON?"
Jon looked back and saw Charlotte heading toward him from
the tuck shop. *Oh, great, now what? I wonder if I can pretend I didn't hear
her...*

"Jon, I need to talk to you. Can you please wait up?"

Too late, she saw me look back.

"Oh, hi, Charlotte." He slowed down and let her catch up with
him. "Actually, I'm just on my way to town. Need anything?"

"No, I just wanted to make sure you heard about the schedule
change?"

"Yeah, I got it."

"Okay, so that means the wide game is right after supper, then,
right?"

"Sure."

"And you're running it, right?"

"Sure, no problem."

"Do you have it ready to go?"

Jon allowed a little bit of exasperation into his tone. "Of course —
it'll be ready to go!"

"Okay, well, if you need anything, let me know sooner than later,
please. I have a supper meeting, so I won't be able to run around and
find things for you last minute."

"Yeah, okay, sure. Whatever. It'll be fine." *Seriously? You don't trust me to run a stupid game?*

Charlotte looked like she wanted to say more, but she just nodded and walked off. Things had been a little tense between Charlotte and him all summer. It seemed like any time he did something not quite perfectly, she would show up and "correct" him. In his books, she was a meddler. Worse, he didn't seem to be able to charm her like he did most of the young female staff. She seemed to see right through him, and that made him feel vulnerable. Not many people could do that.

Man, I still have a bunch to do to get that ready. Shoulda done that this morning when I had time. But I really want to go to town. There should be enough time when I get back, though.

"Jonny!"

Jon saw Leah and Cindy standing by his car waiting for him. Good-looking girls that he didn't mind being seen with, even if their constant chatter set his teeth on edge a bit. He'd told them he would take them to town during their break. It seemed like a good idea at the time.

"Jon, are you ready to go? The kids have been waiting for 15 minutes!"

"Yes, Charlotte, I'm ready to go," he said in a mocking tone. *Except...* "Wait. Can you run and get the pylons for the prison?"

Charlotte made some indistinguishable sound of frustration and ran off to get the pylons. Yeah, he was a little late getting everything together, but it wasn't his fault the run to town had taken so long. Those girls! They had to finish every last bit of their ice cream and then shop for personal items before they could leave town! He'd told them 4:00 and they'd left at almost 4:30! Now he was behind, and everyone thought it was his fault!

"Nicole, can you hand out ribbons to the four teams? Everyone should get two pieces, one for each arm."

Nicole looked up. "What? I'm still cutting these tokens for you. Aren't we supposed to be starting now?"

"Okay, fine! Just bring those tokens as soon as you can. I'll get someone else to hand out ribbons."

"Just give 'em to the team leaders?"

"Yeah, sure. Okay, I'll see you over there."

Jon ran out of the program office, down the stairs, and then turned around and went back inside to grab the ribbon. *Come on. Quit forgetting things!*

Finally, he ran into the gym, which was chaos. Kids were all over the place, and cabin leaders were vainly trying to keep them together. He could sense several of them sighing relief as he ran up onto the stage.

He grabbed the mic, which, of course, was not yet turned on. "Can someone turn this thing on?!"

Finally, it was live. "Hey, everyone, let's get back into our teams and have a seat. It's time for the maaaaaain event!" The gym was surprisingly quiet very quickly. *Give me a microphone and a stage, and they eat out of my hands!*

"All right everybody, we're going to be playing a brand-new game tonight called *Extreme Wolfman*! The rules are a little bit complicated, so I need you to listen carefully." A few boys tittered in the back.

Jon sped through the rules as quickly as he could, hoping he wasn't missing anything. "Okay, any questions?"

A boy, about 11 years old, raised his hand. Jon nodded to him, and he said, "So . . . what do we do?" Lots of kids giggled.

Jon flashed his winning smile and said, "I just explained that. Ask your leader if you don't understand. Anyone else?"

Another young boy near the front, with dyed red hair, raised his hand and began to talk as soon as Jon looked his way. "So, what happens if you tag someone, but they don't *feel* it, and then someone else tags you, and they say you're caught, but you shouldn't be? That's what happened to me last night in the game, and it was totally unfair!"

Jon looked at his watch. "Well, that was a different game. That shouldn't happen in this one because you can only be tagged if you're in the other team's territory."

One of the guy cabin leaders piped up. "But Jon, didn't you say that people could also be tagged in 'no-man's-land'?"

"Well, yeah, but only if they have the Treasure."

"I think you forgot to mention that."

"Oh, yeah, sorry. Okay, yeah, if you have the Treasure, you can be tagged in no-mans-land. Unless you also have the Torch, in which case you would be safe, of course, because you can't be tagged with the Torch."

"But you said the Torch had to be carried separately!" a girl called out.

"Well, yes, but only until the Amulet is recovered. I thought that was clear? And you can't carry the Amulet and the Treasure together, no matter what. And the Amulet gives you safe passage anyway. So, hopefully, that's all clear now because we need to get started. Blue and Yellow will be starting over on the playing field at the far end, and Red and Green will be starting outside right here. Okay, let's hurry to our spots. The bell will sound when it starts. Go!"

The kids started to go when Jon suddenly remembered. "Wait, stop, everyone, one more thing!" Some of the kids had already walked out the door, but Jon continued anyway. "I forgot to mention that only two people can guard the prison, and only one can be a staff person. Okay, go, have fun! I'll ring the bell when it's time to start."

Wow, that was painful. Next time I think we'll play "hide and go seek." Way fewer rules. I hope Nicole got those tokens in place. He hopped off the stage and headed out the door behind the last campers. He caught Charlotte looking at him, but she looked away immediately. *Yeah, okay, fine, so I wasn't as prepared as I could have been. It's Leah's and Cindy's fault, not mine. Quit your meddling, anyway.*

Debriefing

IT DOESN'T MATTER if you are planning a wedding, a fundraising dinner, or a game for a small group of campers, planning well ahead makes a huge difference to its success or failure. Poorly organized events are incredibly frustrating, yet how often do we see this, even at camps, where we do this for a living?!

In the camp setting, we usually know times and events well in advance, and so we have the opportunity to plan well, if we take the time to do so, yet there have been so many times that I have seen events fail for lack of preparation. Occasionally, plans need to change suddenly, but even those unexpected situations can usually be anticipated. "Oh, look, it's raining, and we have nothing for the campers to do!" You're telling me there is no contingency plan for rain, something that, at least where I live, is a rather regular occurrence?! Planning ahead means our program continues seamlessly in most situations, which is great for campers and staff alike.

Here are some basic principles to consider when planning an event of any kind:

1. Know the purpose from the start

Many people would say that games for campers are purely for fun, and if that is the case, well, make it fun! But determine that ahead of planning the event. Decide if this event is to give the campers a hilarious, fun time, or is it to help them bond in their cabin groups? Are we designing it to teach something, such as the food chain or biodiversity? Are we primarily using this activity for exercise or to wear them out before bedtime? Is this an event to honor those who have exceeded expectations or achieved something this week?

There can be many reasons or purposes for an event at camp, and it is vital to know the primary reason for the event before you start planning it, because your purpose will determine many of the choices you make as you begin to plan it. For example, if an activity is supposed to promote teamwork, and the rules of your game make all the campers scatter, that might be something to look at differently.

2. Think through your timeframe and make a flowchart

When I was in college, I was taking a very heavy course load, and I was overwhelmed by all the assignments. The worst thing was that many of them, from different profs, were due on the same days or close together. So I got in the habit each semester of getting a calendar and plotting out not just when assignments were due, but when I would need to start them to get them done on time. Sometimes that meant a project that would only take three to four days had to be started several weeks in advance.

This is the kind of planning that needs to go into big events, too. If Jon was going to go to town, he couldn't be sure how long that would take, so he should have had things in place much earlier. Not only do the preparations need a time frame, but the event itself often needs a flowchart or schedule of some type so that you know what is supposed to be happening when, and who is responsible for each part.

3. Share your plan

As we put a plan together, it is very helpful to talk it through with at least one or two others and get their feedback. This does two things. First, it allows others, with fresh eyes and ears, to think through what you have thought through, and question and clarify how things are going to take place. They will often catch areas you simply haven't considered yet or point out potential problems or inconsistencies.

The second way this helps is that when you begin to explain things to others, you will clarify things in your mind as well. I've often started to explain something to someone and suddenly realized, *Wait, that doesn't work very well!* I think we're often afraid to share our plans because we want to seem more competent by not asking for help, but I have realized over the years in my own life that this is more about arrogance than competency. If we want our plans to succeed, the counsel and help of others is, well, helpful!

4. Strive for excellence

A core value of many organizations is *excellence*. Not *perfection*, as we do expect mistakes from time to time, but if we truly want excellence in our food, our property, our program, and so on, it is going to take more than wishful thinking. We are going to need to work hard, well in advance.

Usually, excellence is found in the details, and some of us hate details! This is another reason it is valuable to work in a team on events. I'm a big-picture kind of guy, and I love coming up with concepts. I can do detail work, but to be honest, it kind of bores me. So, I need to find someone who is passionate about details (they are out there, trust me!), or I need to give myself enough time to slog through them myself. Either way, it takes time and considerable effort.

5. Make a to-do checklist

One of the simplest tools available to us is the good ol' checklist. Simple to create and use, it is your key to success in any planning venture. Even better than a hand-written checklist is one that is saved on your computer because then you can use it repeatedly, adding (or removing) items as need be.

I do this even with my packing list for vacations (using Excel), and each time I go away, I print off a list, make a mark beside each item I need to bring with me, and then check them off as I pack them. It's quick and easy, and in all the travel I've done over the past 20 years using such a list, I can't remember a single time I left the house missing something I had meant to bring. Checklists bring peace to us because a quick glance will tell us we are on track.

Even better than a simple checklist is a time-framed checklist, where you show what needs to be done by when. Sometimes it is as simple as making three columns: "This Week," "Next Week," and "Future." Whenever I feel overwhelmed by a task, I take a few minutes to make a list of what needs to be done and when. Soon, instead of the task controlling me and my emotions, I find I am then in control of the task and my emotions regarding it.

6. Check and double-check

How many times do you send out emails with errors or a missing attachment? Getting in the habit of checking things before they go out can save you a lot of time – and embarrassment. The same goes for games. You needed 15 bandanas. Did you count them out? Okay, let's get someone to count them again, just in case, and throw in an extra couple in case something happens. That extra minute and those extra bandanas could save you from being short and looking disorganized when it's time to play that game.

Sometimes it's great to have a second (short) checklist that you go over just before starting, listing what you need to have with you as you go. I do this all the time for events, and I check that list ten minutes or so before things start. There are many times when I have everything ready to go, but, oops, the pens for the whiteboard are still on my desk, ready to go, but not yet taken. Okay, let's grab them and the eraser before I head over. Again, the principle here is striving for excellence. If you are using any kind of electronics such as a sound system or PowerPoint, make sure they are checked well ahead of time and then again a few minutes before you start. So many great plans fail because something isn't working with the A/V. It doesn't have to be that way if you plan ahead.

7. Have contingency plans

Many things come up last minute that you can anticipate and plan around. For example, it is very hard with a new game to know exactly how long it is going to run unless you put time considerations in the rules. Games with open-ended goals, like capture the flag, can have an extra rule such as, "the game goes until either the flag is captured or 60 minutes elapse." In those kinds of games, you also need a plan for what happens if the flag is captured in a short time. Is there time to play again (with a shorter end-time now), or do you have a different activity that is ready to go, just in case?

It is also vital to have a backup plan in case there is rain or something else comes up making it impossible or inappropriate to go with Plan A. The truth is, in some cases you will need a Plan B *and* a Plan C. What happens if you are doing a play and someone suddenly gets sick or has to leave camp for personal reasons? Hopefully, you have an understudy or a second cast, someone who can fill in at a moment's notice. Something happens in the kitchen, and the food is suddenly going to be half an hour late. Do we have plans for what to do with the campers? These things happen and are fairly easy to anticipate. What's the plan? Is it written down? Have the people who need to know about it been informed?

8. Delegate wisely

Some people seem to think that asking for help shows inadequacy, so they try to do everything on their own. The trouble is, as I have hinted earlier, we all have different gifts and abilities. I love creative thinkers, but they can be poor with details. And late. Everyone is good at certain things, so it is great to have a team of people who are differently skilled and diverse in their opinions, especially if they are part of the initial planning stages.

Delegation is never about "passing the buck." In fact, proper delegation means *you* are still responsible to see that it is done. When there are skills to be learned, delegation should follow a pattern like this:

1. I do it; you watch
2. I do it; you help
3. You do it; I help
4. You do it; I watch
5. You do it and report to me

Notice that the task I am delegating is still ultimately my responsibility. That is until or if it gets transferred to someone else's job description.

When delegating, instructions should be clear and written down if possible. There should be a time-frame involved, as in, "I need these no later than 3:00, please." Delegation is not simply about passing work to others; rather see it as a tool to train and develop others to learn to do what you already do well. In some cases, you will also delegate to cover areas you simply are not good at.

9. Communicate clearly

Many of the most wonderful plans in the world have failed simply because of miscommunication. Someone plans a beautiful dinner for you, but you show up a day late because either they sent the information incorrectly, or you wrote it down incorrectly. True communication only happens when the intended message is correctly received by the intended person(s).

At camp, the breakdown often occurs in the explanations of the rules of a game or activity. Usually, it is best for the leaders helping to run a game to understand it *before* it is explained to the campers. If the game is at all complicated, written instructions are usually best. This helps everyone to be on the same page (literally and figuratively), and it saves a lot of grief that comes when people are interpreting rules differently.

As much as you can, write things out clearly and succinctly, and try to avoid convoluted rules or explanations. Before you explain the rules to the campers, decide what the most important things are for them to know and if there is anything you can leave out. I believe in always having the rules written out in front of you in numbered points so that you can be sure you are not missing anything. But you should also practice giving the rules ahead of time, so you aren't simply reading them in a monotone!

Wherever possible, weave a story into the rules of your game and connect it to your week's theme if you have one. This will help make the rules more interesting and give people a context by which to remember them.

10. Expect last minute issues

Stuff happens. Even when you plan incredibly well, something can come up at the last minute to make things suddenly need to be changed. For that reason alone, be completely ready to go *at least* ten minutes before the event is supposed to start (or much longer if it is a big event). This gives you time to adapt when someone who you were counting on is stuck in traffic, or the equipment you were going to use is suddenly missing or not working.

This is true in life in general. We leave margins on our pages so we can add things as needed, but if we write to all the edges, this is impossible. It is the same in life – if it takes ten minutes to get to work, and you give yourself exactly ten minutes to get there, what happens when an accident blocks a road? You've left no room for it, and you'll be late, or you now have to speed, potentially getting a ticket or causing an accident. This goes the same with budgeting money as well as time. Always leave room for those things that can come up – because they often will.

11. Take time afterward to evaluate

I cannot stress enough how valuable it is to take a bit of time after an activity or event and evaluate how it went, preferably with others who were involved. This may not be necessary if you are not planning to do the event again (like your wedding – hopefully), but if you will be running it again, you should always write down a few notes for next time. Unless it went absolutely perfectly, in which case you should just give yourself and your team gold stars and go make a living doing that event.

However, for mortals like me, there are usually a few things we could have been done better. The problem is, I think I will remember those things for next time, but by the time it rolls around again, I have forgotten. It is shameful to make the same mistake twice! Even if there aren't glaring problems or errors, ask yourself and your team, were there things we could have done better? How can we make this more understandable and more fun?

Okay, some of you are probably thinking that this whole process takes a ton of work, and you are right, at least for the first time or two. But in the long run, this type of rigorous thinking and planning saves a lot of time, effort, and stress on everyone. And it leads to excellence.

"But I'm only running *Capture the Flag*, and I've done it a hundred times." Okay, that's fine, and maybe you've perfected the leading of that one game. But, hopefully, you're going to change it up and try new things sometimes; otherwise, you probably should find someone a little more creative to be in charge! And when you do try something new, follow these principles, or adapt them to your style, and you will likely find that things run a lot more smoothly. After all, it's for the campers, and they are worth the effort!

Discussion Questions

1. Can you think of a time when something wasn't organized very well at camp? How did it make you feel?

2. Do you think Charlotte is "meddling" in Jon's work? Why or why not?

3. Give at least five things Jon could have done differently to make the game run more smoothly.

4. Do you think campers should be expected to wait for camp leaders to get things ready? What messages are we sending when we are not ready for them on time?

5. Would you say that you think things through and plan before starting them, or are you more of a "fly by the seat of your pants" kind of person? What are some benefits of planning ahead?

6. Do you ever use checklists to help keep on track? How do they work for you? If you don't use them, what is keeping you from doing that?

7. Why are contingency plans important? How can you anticipate what *might* go wrong?

8. What place does evaluation have in an event? Why is it helpful?

CHAPTER 9

Melchizedek & Apocalyptic Scripture
Teaching God's Word

"OKAY, BOYS, let's quiet down now!" Jon felt the sting of irony that he was yelling so loudly for everyone to be quiet. *Would you guys just* shut up*!*

It had been a rough few days for Jon with his cabin, and he couldn't figure out why. *I've practically let them do whatever they wanted, so I should be their best friend by now! But the little ingrates still won't listen to me.* All week he'd been struggling to get them to pay attention when he did his devotional just before bed, but tonight was even worse than usual.

"I mean it! Shut - your - mouths! Okay? Just settle down! This is your last warning, and then it'll be no pillow fight tomorrow!"

The boys began to quiet down a little, but Joey and Curtis were still arguing about something to do with a dirty shoe print on Joey's bed.

"Seriously guys, I shouldn't have to yell. Okay, like I said – five minutes ago! – grab your Bibles. No, never mind, that'll take too long. Let me just read you a couple of Bible verses." He flipped through his huge study Bible to a bookmarked passage. "Okay, this is from Hebrews chapter 7. Listen carefully so that you can answer some questions." He looked down at his Bible and began to read:

> So if the priesthood of Levi, on which the law was based, could have achieved the perfection God intended, why did God need

to establish a different priesthood, with a priest in the order of Melchizedek instead of the order of Levi and Aaron? And if the priesthood is changed, the law must also be changed to permit it. For the priest we are talking about belongs to a different tribe, whose members have never served at the altar as priests. What I mean is, our Lord came from the tribe of Judah, and Moses never mentioned priests coming from that tribe. This change has been made very clear since a different priest, who is like Melchizedek, has appeared. Jesus became a priest, not by meeting the physical requirement of belonging to the tribe of Levi, but by the power of a life that cannot be destroyed. And the psalmist pointed this out when he prophesied, "You are a priest forever in the order of Melchizedek."

Jon finished and looked around. Most of the guys were staring off anywhere but at him. *Man, these guys are spiritually dim. They need a LOT of teaching. This could take a while.*

"Okay, so, who was this passage about?"

Nobody answered. "Tim, who was this about?"

Tim screwed up his ten-year-old face and then gave out a big yawn. "I dunno. Mel Kuzak somebody?"

"*Melchizedek*. That's right. He was a priest, but not a Levitical priest like Aaron's descendants. And that's really important to understand. So, who did the passage say was like Melchizedek? Brian?"

Brian shrugged and looked at the shoelace he was playing with.

"Caleb? You know this."

Caleb looked up and said, "What?" *Seriously, Caleb, pay attention, you zombie!*

"Never mind, Caleb, just keep sleeping over there. Look you guys, this is important! *Jesus* is like Melchizedek, a priest who would live *forever*. So, when we put our trust in Him, it's like we can trust Him with our lives because He rose from the dead. How cool is that?"

Joey piped up. "Hey, Jon?"

"Yeah." *Finally, somebody with a question.*

"Can we go to bed now?"

You little punk. Jon felt his face growing hot. "No! Not until you guys learn about Melchizedek and how he foreshadows the priesthood of Jesus! Why can't you guys just pay attention and learn?! Even in chapel, you guys just ignore the speaker, I can tell!"

Most of the boys looked a little scared of Jon's outburst, and Tim looked like he might cry. There was an awkward silence, until Caleb said, "I pay attention. He was talking about how God is like a dad who loves us and looks for us down the road when we mess up and get lost and stuff."

"Yeah, okay. Good job, Caleb. I'm glad *somebody* was listening this morning!"

Caleb looked up and cocked his head slightly. "Do you think God is like a dad, Jon? I don't even know my dad."

Jon wanted to get back on track quickly before he lost them. "Sure, he is, Caleb. Yeah, just like a dad. But that's not what *this* passage is about. Let's keep on subject. Right now, we're talking about Melchizedek. Okay?"

Caleb shrugged and looked away, a small tear forming in the corner of his eye.

"All right you guys, three more questions on this passage, and then we'll turn to Genesis 14 and find out who this Melchizedek guy really was. All right, Connor, can you tell us…"

"Excuse me, Charlotte, can I talk to you for a minute?" Madison poked her head into the program office, not wanting to go in and disturb anyone.

"Oh, hey, Maddy! Sure, let me just finish this up. Come on in and sit down, and I'll be with you in just a minute." Charlotte turned back to her computer and continued typing up an email.

Madison squeezed in through the half-open door and sat down on the chair facing Charlotte's desk. *Wow, messy place! But I guess there's a lot going on in here. Kind of expected an organized person like Charlotte would be a little cleaner in her office, but I'll bet she knows where to find things.*

"Sorry about the mess," Charlotte said, looking up from her computer as if reading Madison's mind. "I'm a little behind, so guess what doesn't get done?" She grinned sheepishly at Madison.

"I'm sorry. If you're too busy to talk, I can come back later…"

"Oh, no, don't worry about it. Now is just fine. These piles of work aren't going anywhere, and I'd rather talk to you anyway. Shall we go for a walk?"

"Uh, it's a little windy, and I need to go soon, too. I just wondered if you could help me figure out what to say to my kids tonight."

"You mean for your devotional time with them?"

Madison nodded. "Yeah, I just don't feel like the one from the cabin leader book is really where I want to go with these girls tonight."

"Okay, well, what's going on to make you feel that way?" Charlotte leaned back in her chair. Madison noted she looked tired, and dark circles were showing under her eyes. *I guess I'm not the only one exhausted around here.*

"Well, the devo tonight is supposed to be on God's love, but I feel like these girls all get that already. Well, mostly, anyway. They all say they are Christians, so I'd like to talk to them more about making right choices that will help them grow as believers."

"Sure, yeah, that's a great idea. Totally makes sense. Have you chosen your text?"

"Sort of. I looked up in my concordance a whole bunch of verses that have to do with growing, and I think I could kind of string them together to make it work."

Charlotte readjusted in her chair, warming to the topic. "Well, 'topically' is one way to do it. Of course, the main danger in that method is that it is easy to accidentally take verses out of context."

"What do you mean?"

"Okay, well, the Bible was inspired by God, right, so every word is what He wanted to be written down. But He didn't purely *dictate* it to the writers. Rather, He used their personalities and situations to allow them to write things to *specific* audiences who were facing *particular* circumstances. Also, different types of literature in the Bible use symbolism and metaphors, so they may not be meant literally, like in poetry or in the apocalyptic books. You following?"

Madison's brow furled, and Charlotte could tell she was concentrating and thinking about what she was saying. "Yeah, I think so." *English, please? Apoca-what?*

"So, when we read the Bible, verses aren't meant to be read apart from their *contexts*. For example, in the book of Philippians, Paul writes: 'For I can do everything through Christ, who gives me strength.' What does he seem to mean by that?"

Madison shrugged. "I guess he meant the world was full of endless possibilities to him, that he could try anything and succeed as long as he did it in the power of Jesus?"

Charlotte grabbed her Bible from under a stack of papers and began to flip toward the back. "That sounds good, and it *is* true that if God wants us to do something, He'll give us the power and strength to do it." She paused momentarily while she found the passage.

"But in this *particular* verse, when we understand who Paul's audience is, his own personal situation – he's stuck in prison – and we read the verses surrounding that one verse, we see a different picture. Paul is talking about the generosity of the Philippian church and how they had sent money to help meet his needs. He says in verse 12, the verse before, 'I know how to live on almost nothing or with everything. I have learned the secret of living in every situation, whether it is with a full stomach or empty, with plenty or little.' So, when he says he can 'do everything,' he's talking about being *content* in all situations."

Madison nodded, impressed. "Okay, wow. Why didn't I know that?" *I'm an idiot! Everyone must know that except me!*

"Probably because, like I said, you've heard that verse by itself a lot, or maybe you've even been taught that verse out of context. The real danger of not knowing the context of a verse is that it allows people to pick and choose what they want to believe, instead of receiving 'the whole counsel of God.'"

"But I've never been to Bible school, so how am I supposed to know this stuff? How can I know if I'm getting the context right? Do I have to leave it to the 'experts'?" Madison was starting to look and sound defeated.

"Oh, no, not at all. Good Bible training helps, no doubt, but any one of us can read God's Word and understand it if we take it seriously and put a bit of effort into it. A couple of things I try to do is read through the Bible every couple of years and also listen to online sermons or podcasts from great preachers who teach through the Bible, book by book. Then I'm constantly learning context and understanding how it all fits together."

"You read through the *whole* Bible?" *Wow, she must be really spiritual.*

"Oh, come on, Maddy, it only takes about 15 minutes per day to read it all in one year. I can give you a reading plan if you want, or they're easy to find online."

"Maybe... but what do I do about tonight? I can't read it all before tonight! How am I supposed to know if the verses I chose are 'in context,' like you said?

Charlotte was silent for a moment while she thought. "Hmm. Well, the best thing then would be to choose a passage that is reasonably short and straight-forward and build it from there. I did a devo last summer on Psalm 1. It's a pretty cool – and short – psalm that shows the huge difference our choices make. It says that those who meditate on God's Word are like trees growing by a river, but those who choose evil are like chaff that blows away."

"Can I see your Bible for a second?" Charlotte nodded and passed it over her desk. Madison flipped to Psalm 1 while Charlotte continued. *Good thing I know where the Psalms are!*

"In order to make it easy for the kids to understand, I did an object lesson with a healthy plant and a dry, brown leaf. I think it helped them to see which kind of life they would rather live."

Madison was quiet while she read the short Psalm. Then she looked up and said, "Hey, that's pretty good. I could see making this work. But . . . what's the context?"

Charlotte smiled. "Smart question! Would you like me to give you notes from my lesson? I had used a few commentaries to get a good grip on all that."

"Sure! That would be great!"

"And if you have time, or if you want to continue it tomorrow, you could always read John 15:1-8, which talks about being connected to Jesus, the True Vine, and how abiding in Jesus allows us to bear good fruit. Just a thought. Actually, I think I have notes on that one as well." Charlotte began to shuffle through her filing cabinet to find the lessons she had done.

"Thanks, Charlotte! And I'll keep in mind what you said about using verses out of context, too."

"Oh, here it is. Here you go. Yeah, it's not that you can't use a single verse here and there, it's just that you need to make sure that you at least know a little bit about where it's coming from. That'll come with time and study. But if you have any questions, you know where to find me."

Madison nodded and got up to leave. "Okay, thanks so much! I'll give it a try. See you later!" *I sure hope I can do this, but at least now I know where to start. Lord? Help?*

Debriefing

TEACHING KIDS from God's Word is one of the most amazing privileges you can have. It is like you are bringing a treasure chest to these kids, opening it, and offering them riches beyond their wildest dreams. Teaching God's Word is like breathing Life into them, like giving food to someone starving, or like providing cool water for someone who is dying of thirst. True, many will not recognize it as such, but some will, and you will have the opportunity to help them come face to face with the Lord of the Universe, the One who can transform their whole existence and give them Eternal Life.

But what does it take to become a good teacher of the Word, especially if you have had little or no biblical training? Here are some thoughts that may be helpful:

1. Immerse yourself in God's Word.

There is no substitute for studying God's Word. I am amazed at how few Christians spend time in God's Word daily. I find it very sad as I regularly observe Christians, in person and on social media, giving opinions that are informed by the world and not by Scripture. To grow as a Christian and to be effective in your faith, you must get to know God through His Word. Deuteronomy 6:4-9, the famous "Shema" passage, recited daily by Jews for many centuries, says this:

> Listen, O Israel! The Lord is our God, the Lord alone. And you must love the Lord your God with all your heart, all your soul, and all your strength. And you must commit yourselves wholeheartedly to these commands that I am giving you today. Repeat them again and again to your children. Talk about them when you are at home and when you are on the road, when you are going to bed and when you are getting up. Tie them to your

hands and wear them on your forehead as reminders. Write them on the doorposts of your house and on your gates.

Do you get that? We are to teach God's Word to each other, talk about it, write it down – make it a focus of every day and of everything we do. Second Timothy 2:15 says,

> Work hard so you can present yourself to God and receive his approval. Be a good worker, one who does not need to be ashamed and who correctly explains the word of truth.

Paul was encouraging Timothy to work hard at being someone who knows God's Word and can explain it correctly. That's important for all of us, especially if we are in a position to teach others, as Timothy was.

Dozens of other passages, such as Psalm 1, Psalm 19, and Psalm 119:105 come quickly to my head as I write this. There are so many Scriptures that tell us the benefits of meditating on God's Word and the incredible benefits and blessings that come from it. Romans 12:2 tells us that the way we are to be *transformed* is by the renewing of our minds. The implication is that we need to be constantly thinking about God's Words, mulling them over in our heads, like a cow chews its cud.

Honestly, there is no substitute, no shortcut to knowing the mind, heart, and counsel of the Lord. Read through the Bible cover to cover every two or three years, but also spend time daily reading shorter passages and praying through them and memorizing them. God's Words will be a comfort to you in times of need and the sword you need to defend yourself against the Enemy's attacks (see Jesus' battle strategy in Matthew 4). They will guide your mind and actions and therefore become the basis for your character. The best time to plant a tree is twenty years ago; the second-best time is right now. If you aren't meditating on God's Word daily, start today!

2. Use a logical and simple process to plan.

If you are planning a Bible study from scratch, here is a relatively simple process to use that will help you progress through a passage:

- Choose a passage, or possibly just a verse or two, based on what you want to teach, or something God has put on your heart.

- Spend some time reading, re-reading, and studying the verses so that you understand them very well. Make sure you understand the bigger context (e.g., the whole book), the specific context (the verses surrounding it), and what all the words mean in English. What is the author of this book trying to convey to his original audience? What is the main lesson here? If you are unsure, use tools to help you (see point #3 below).

- Choose questions that bring out the *content*, *meaning*, and *application*. In other words, you are asking what this passage is *saying*, what this passage *means*, and *how* we should live now that we understand it. Generally, choose questions that require campers to think, ones to which they can't simply answer "yes" or "no." You want them to wrestle with the passage.

- Develop illustrations, object lessons, stories from real life, and so on to bring home the main point of the passage.

- As time allows, see if there are other Scripture passages that help to understand the one you chose. Make sure you understand the basic context of those verses and their meaning. Scripture is often the best interpreter of other Scripture.

- Check the whole lesson plan to ensure it flows logically, is understandable, and stays on the main point. Does this lesson move kids to follow Jesus, or is it just information?

- Don't be afraid to ask someone who is a little more experienced than you are with God's Word about anything you might be unsure of. There are usually lots of people who can help.

3. Use tools if they are available.

Okay, so maybe you aren't a Bible scholar. That's fine because you can learn from those who *are* scholars, those who have spent countless hours studying the passages you will want to teach. The best tool for teaching the Bible is the Bible itself, read in several solid versions when possible. I would suggest the second-best tool is a good study Bible, where there are notes right below the passage, helping you get the gist of what is being taught. But don't just read the study notes for a given passage, read the full introduction to the book you are studying. And read the verses and notes on the verses surrounding the passage you are teaching.

Besides those simple tools, there are entire books called "commentaries," that dissect passages verse by verse, phrase by phrase, or even word by word. Some of these are quite complex, but others are a lot easier to read. For example, check out the *Wiersbe Bible Commentary*, which can be purchased on Amazon in a couple of huge volumes, covering the whole Bible, or in many smaller volumes (the *BE* series), covering individual books of the Bible.

There are also tools to look up individual words in the original languages, since the Bible was originally written mainly in Hebrew (Old Testament) and Greek (New Testament). Sometimes the nuance of a word or phrase can significantly alter the meaning of a passage. But even using a plain English dictionary will help you at least understand the words in a passage you are studying. Talk to your pastor or a more mature Christian, and they can probably help you find tools that will be suitable for your level of education and experience.

4. Focus on relatively clear passages.

This all sounds like a lot of work, I'm sure, and I don't want to minimize that. Good Bible study takes time and work, and you may not have time at camp to do as much as a passage requires. That's why it is often wise to stick to passages that are a little more straightforward. Not only is this helpful for you in preparing to teach a passage, but it is also better for your campers who will not usually be ready for the weightier passages. Maybe avoid teaching about Melchizedek, for starters!

Generally speaking, much of the Old Testament will be harder to teach. It is very important that you have a working knowledge of the Old Testament, as it is the basis for almost everything we read in the New Testament. However, most of the Old Testament takes a lot of studying to understand, since we are so far removed from those times and because they are so "Jewish" in flavor. Popular verses like

Jeremiah 29:11 are often used out of context, without any consideration to the verses that surround them or the situations in which the people of God found themselves.

There are also great stories in the Old Testament, and these can be helpful for moral teaching, but be aware that stories like David and Goliath also have historical settings and theological implications that can easily be missed on the surface. Poetic books like the Psalms and Proverbs can be quite straightforward, and of course, parts of Genesis can help campers get a good basis for the "rest of the story." However, as mentioned below, many of these passages are hard to connect directly to the gospel message, which the campers so badly need to hear and understand.

5. Keep the Gospel central.

Don't forget to "keep the main thing the main thing." While it is fun to start talking about end times and issues we think the campers are interested in, the main two things we should be concerned about teaching are how to begin a relationship with God and how to grow in that relationship (evangelism and discipleship). Our teaching should revolve around the story of Jesus, the teachings by Jesus, and the later teachings about what Jesus accomplished on the cross and through His resurrection. Those are the transformative teachings campers need, even if you have campers who have grown up learning about Jesus.

So, teach regularly from Matthew, Mark, Luke, and John. Use Acts to show the growth and persecution of the early church. Use the New Testament epistles (letters) to teach about doctrine and discipleship. Continually bring the campers back to the sacrifice of Jesus and their need to put their faith in Him and live for Him in their daily lives.

6. Use easily accessible resources to keep learning.

In this age of information, it is easy to find online courses and sermons that will help ground you in the Word and help you grow in your knowledge and understanding of God's Word. Take an Alpha program for starters (or something similar), go to conferences, listen to podcasts from great preachers, read books by great Christian authors. I would also recommend that anyone serious about following Jesus should spend at least a year in a Christian school, like a Capernwray or a Bible college.

7. Make use of the people around you.

Just like Charlotte passed her Psalm 1 notes on to Madison, there are mature Christians around you at camp who will have good ideas and good resources for you to use. They can show you where to find Bible studies that are already prepared for you, and you can also find those things online or in a Christian bookstore. Don't be afraid to ask! But one little suggestion here: anytime you use someone else's material, be sure to spend a good amount of time studying it and making it your own. Adapt it to your style and to the needs and purposes of your time with your campers.

8. Keep the lesson simple.

Studying the Bible to teach it to others can feel overwhelming, but it doesn't need to be. Determine the main point of a passage you want to teach, and use every tool you can to drive that one point home.

Don't try to teach too much in one session. For example, when teaching the gospel, you can teach each of these points over several sessions:

a) God created us and loves us.

b) We have gone astray by sinning against Him.

c) Jesus died on the cross to pay the penalty for our sins.

d) We can be forgiven and receive eternal life by putting our trust in Him.

Each one of those points can be illustrated in many ways and from many passages, but stick to that one point for your whole time. Also see Appendix A, "A Simple Gospel Presentation," where I have listed several verses for the above points and presented it in an easy and accessible way.

9. Don't be afraid of not knowing the answer.

After decades of studying God's Word and earning a couple of theological degrees, I can still be stumped by campers' questions. Rather than pretending I know, I simply tell them that they have asked a great question, and I will get back to them with the answer soon. It's okay not to know everything, and it is a simple thing to go and seek the answer from someone who does know.

10. Consider learning outcomes.

Always ask *why* you are doing what you are doing. I mean that in all of life, but also in leading a devotional or Bible study. Is the goal to pass on information, or is it to see kids learn and grow? If it is the latter (i.e., you've been paying attention so far!), you want the campers to do as much self-discovery as possible. Have them be in their Bibles, flipping through pages, finding things, reading it for themselves, asking questions, and so on. The point is to never just "put in time," fill their minds with facts, or entertain them. What we want is to lead them on a treasure hunt, where the reward is eternal life in Jesus.

11. Keep on track . . . unless you shouldn't.

Try not to get sidetracked by questions and comments that have nothing to do with the lesson. That is, unless you receive a serious question that may lead to a better lesson. Sometimes we get thrown off-track much too easily, and sometimes it's our own fault for taking rabbit trails about things we suddenly think of that don't really add to what we're teaching. We need to be very deliberate and focused.

However, when a camper asks something from the heart, you have to make a choice: do I deal with this now and sacrifice the lesson I was planning on, or do I acknowledge the validity of the question and promise to come back to it at another time? That is not always an easy choice, but either way, don't ignore those opportunities when they come – like Jon did in our story.

12. Pray!

If the point of camp is seeing kids transformed by the power of God, then guess what? It's not up to you to make that happen! If it is truly only by the power of the Holy Spirit that kids will change, then we had better be on our knees praying for God to work in the lives of these kids. That especially holds true when we are teaching God's Word.

Pray that God would lead you to a passage they need to hear, pray that He would open their eyes and ears to the truth of the Word, and pray that you would speak words that would help the kids understand. In the end, you may not *feel* like you have accomplished much, but if you are faithfully opening God's Word to your campers, He will be making changes in their lives, even if you don't see it. Trust Him!

As Paul wrote to his protégé, Timothy, in 2 Timothy 4:1-2:

> I solemnly urge you in the presence of God and Christ Jesus, who will someday judge the living and the dead when he comes to set up his Kingdom: Preach the word of God. Be prepared, whether the time is favorable or not. Patiently correct, rebuke, and encourage your people with good teaching.

It is an incredible privilege and responsibility to teach God's Word. Be a wise, studied, and Spirit-filled teacher.

Discussion Questions

1. Why do you think Jon would lead a Bible study on Melchizedek?

2. Besides a poor choice of passage, what else did Jon do poorly in his approach?

3. What opportunity did Jon miss with Caleb? What would you have done?

4. Do you ever feel like you don't know enough to teach kids from the Bible? Is there ever an arrival point where someone now knows enough? Why or why not?

5. What kind of tools can you use to better understand a passage you are reading?

6. What are the three kinds of questions that can help people understand a Bible passage?

7. What kind of object lesson or illustration could you use to teach campers about Jesus' sacrifice on the cross?

8. If you agree that it is important to immerse ourselves in God's Word, what will you do to develop better disciplines for studying it? When will you start?

CHAPTER 10

Dangers in the Dark
Failing Forward

T HE MOON WAS SHINING DIMLY through the cloud cover, providing the scantest light. Madison's ears strained to determine what that noise was she thought she could hear. From her vantage point behind the bushes, she could see almost nothing of where they were trying to get. *Footsteps. Those are footsteps.* A small light flickered in the same direction the noise came from. Sudden fear of discovery flowed through her.

The game was almost over, and they had failed miserably at getting anywhere near their target, usually because one of her girls would do something stupid, like running right into a guard and almost knocking him over. Or calling to each other, instantly giving away their position. They weren't exactly the subtlest group of kids she'd ever worked with. But *finally*, by sheer luck, they had walked practically into the enemy base without getting caught. Their goal was within reach, just on the other side of those bushes.

Madison continued to listen, and the footsteps stopped. Silence. Then, thankfully, they started to move away from the girls' position. Okay, just a few more seconds, and they would have a chance to run for it. From a few feet away, she could just barely see the girls in her cabin. She gestured to them to watch her for the signal to run. *Okay, here we go. Now or never... Ready, and...*

"Stop touching me!" Chelsea said loudly. "I didn't!" *That must be Chloe.* "Quiet!" Madison whispered to them, but it was too late. Lights suddenly flickered all around them, and heavy footsteps got louder.

"Run for it!" Madison called out, as she stood up and navigated her way around the bushes.

Two guards suddenly blocked her path, and another one came up quickly behind them.

"Ha!" said one of them. "That's where you guys went! I was following you for a while, but then I got busy with another cabin sneaking around over by the creek. If you hadn't given away your position, you might have made it!"

"Thanks a lot, Chelsea!" muttered one of the girls, followed by similar comments by the others.

"Shut up!" exclaimed Chelsea. "You're such a pain. It's a stupid game anyway. Can we go back now?"

"I suppose we might as well," sighed Madison. "It's almost over anyway." Just then, the bell sounded. "Yup, there you go. You girls are a real delight."

It had been one of those weeks for Madison. Girls that simply didn't like each other and resisted all her efforts to help them have a good time. She'd already had to take Chelsea aside three times, twice for picking on girls in the cabin, and once for talking back to her. There was just something about Chelsea that grated on her, and she didn't know what to do about it.

But as much as it would be satisfying to blame her troubles on Chelsea, Madison knew she wasn't the only problem child in the cabin. Chloe was a pest – she just *asked* for Chelsea to pick on her, like she badly needed the attention. And Hannah was a constant whiner. No matter what happened, it wasn't fair, or she had to sigh or roll her eyes (usually both at the same time).

The trouble was, even with the kids who weren't a pain, Madison wasn't nearly as patient as she had been earlier in the summer. This was her third week in a row of counseling, and she was exhausted. She wasn't even supposed to be in the cabin this week. That was until two others got sick.

Madison reflected on her week as she led her girls back to the cabin. *Yeah, I'm not even supposed to be their cabin leader this week. What a mistake it was to put me with them. What a terrible bunch of kids! I've tried so hard to connect with them, but it just doesn't work. What a waste of time.*

Then, as often happened, Madison started getting that irksome feeling inside. She tried to ignore it, but it wouldn't go away. *Really, Lord? I'm being selfish? All I've done this summer has been for these kids. Couldn't I get a little something back? Couldn't I just get some cooperative kids for a change?*

They continued to trudge along the path, and now there were campers and cabin leaders all around them, some with flashlights, some without, most of them talking loudly and excitedly, sharing successes, near misses, and hilarious events from the past hour. *Listen to how happy everyone else's cabin is, Lord! Why can't mine have better attitudes?*

How's your attitude, Maddy? Madison stopped in her tracks and was bumped by the girl behind her. "What are you *doing*?" asked Chelsea, who had bumped her. Of course, it would be Chelsea.

"Sorry, just had to stop for a second." *What was that? Was that in my mind, or did I hear that? How's my attitude? Well, yeah, not so good.* She thought about that for a while, as she walked over the playing field now. *Please forgive me, Lord. I haven't exactly been my best this week. Not very patient. Or loving. Or gentle. I'm just so tired!*

Madison felt like God was reminding her that her strength was in Him. *Yes, Lord, I'm so sorry I've been trying to do it on my own. Please give me the strength to love these girls the way you do or even a fraction of how much You do. And thank you for being patient with me when I mess up. Like today. And most days.*

A small seed of hope began to bud in her heart as she prayed, and Madison began to feel like it was all going to be okay. She knew she had to apologize to her girls for her attitude, and even if they didn't change for the rest of the week, she decided she would still love them with the love she continued to receive from Jesus, each day. *I know You never promised it would be easy, Lord, but You did promise to be with me through these storms. I choose to trust You.*

"Easy does it, fellows," Jon whispered, as he giggled quietly to himself. *Oh, man, is old Brucey going to wet himself over this one!*

The first couple of times the podium went missing had been hilarious. It was fun watching their immense speaker get all flustered when he arrived and had to use a regular music stand instead of the sturdy, wooden podium that he loved to lean on with his massive bulk. Nothing against him, really – he was a fine speaker, but stealing the podium under the auspices of the "Podium Liberation Organization" was just too good to pass up.

"Come on, Jon, help me pull it up!" David whispered into the darkness. Jon put his flashlight down so that it would still light up tree branches and grabbed the rope with David. Together, they managed to get the podium strung up about fifteen feet off the ground before Jon tied it off. Jon looked up and saw it swinging back and forth gently, a thick noose around its "neck."

"Perfect!" Jon said quietly. "Let's go deliver the note." They'd forgotten to drop it off when they stole the podium. The note, of course, was brilliant, even if they hadn't been. It read: "I can't take it any longer. Life is no longer worth living. I've been leaned on and abused too many times, and enough is enough. Give my regrets to any who care. This is my final liberation. – Your Favorite Podium."

Jon and David crept along outside the chapel and toward the back door. A dog barked, causing both of them to jump. Jon looked at David and laughed. Then he whispered, "You look like you've seen a ghost, Davey!"

"Shut up, or we're gonna get caught. Why do I listen to you?"

"You've been asking that for years. I make your life interesting." The dog barked again, and they could hear it straining against its chain. It was the "camp dog," a big Yellow Labrador. It was gentle as could be with children, but it took its role as a guard dog seriously. Jon had forgotten that it was usually outside at night.

They found the back door, opened it, and crept in, down the hallway to the front. Jon found the note in his back pocket and put it on the stage, where it couldn't be missed. Smiling, inside and out, they crept back down the aisle.

Suddenly, the main lights came on, and they were momentarily blinded. Then they saw Bruce, with green slippers, a blue robe, and very messy hair, looking extremely unimpressed.

"Busted," Bruce said, shaking his head. "Boy, I've always wanted to be in the right place, at the right time, to catch you in one of your pranks, but now that I'm here, it just makes me sick." He looked at the boys and shook his head again. The silence spoke more loudly than his words had.

Jon finally spoke up. "Bruce, I'm so sorry we woke you up. I - I can explain." *No, I can't. I've got nothing. Think. Think.*

"David, you can go to bed. I want you in my office right after staff meeting tomorrow morning. You can go." David glared angrily at Jon as if it was all his fault, and wandered off, out the back door.

"Look, Bruce, it was just a harmless joke. I know we shouldn't be up this late, but really, we're not hurting anyone. It won't happen again."

"Jon, I've heard all of your excuses, time after time. I'm tired, and I really don't want to deal with this tonight, but I'm going to. You've been ignoring the rules all summer and causing others to break rules as well. You've lied to me several times – yes, I know about the shaving cream, the underwear up the flagpole, the food dye in the showers, and a number of other little episodes – and this has got to stop."

Jon wasn't sure if Bruce's words or his obvious disappointment were worse. He respected Bruce, and he really didn't want to let him down. But he'd gotten out of worse situations before, and he just had to play it carefully and as contritely as possible.

"Oh, man, you're so right, Bruce. I am just such a jerk! You should probably put me on probation or something! I am *so* sorry." Jon tried to look as broken up about it as he could.

Bruce again shook his head, his eyes very sad. "No, that's not going to do it this time, Jon. I'm sending you home. For the rest of this week and all next week, and then we'll go from there."

Jon froze. He couldn't believe his ears. *Home? Oh, man, no way. Mom's going to kill me!*

"You can't be serious, Bruce? Really? Look, I'll improve, really, I will. I'll – look, let me stay, and I'll head up the bathroom cleaning every night. I'll do whatever you want, just, please, don't send me home."

Bruce sat down on the chair he'd been leaning on. "Jon, it's been a long summer, and we have three and a half weeks to go. I'm sending you home to think about your attitude. I want you to really look inside and ask yourself *why* you come to camp. You act like it's just a big party, and you're the guest of honor. Most of the rest of the staff are here because we truly care about kids, and each other, and we want to see lives transformed. Jon, you're here for *yourself*! Sure, you can be good with kids, and you're a pretty good activity leader, but when push comes to shove, you regularly put yourself ahead of anything and everyone else. You think you are above the rules, and I honestly believe that it's a spiritual issue. You aren't here to serve God!"

Jon was stunned. No one had called him out like that in years. Well, maybe his mom, but she was, well, his mom. And she often let her love for him blind her to half the things he was up to at home.

"I'm sorry, Bruce. You're right. I'm way off base here. Maybe we should talk about this in the morning…"

Bruce sadly shook his head and continued, "Jon, let me ask you this, and don't give me any crap: where are you at with your relationship with God?"

Jon thought for a moment. *What do I say? I believe. I asked Jesus into my heart at camp, what, eight years ago? But honestly?* "I don't know, Bruce. Kind of okay, I guess. I honestly don't think about it much. I mean, I'm a Christian and all that, and I think God's okay with most of what I do. He loves me." *Even if you don't.*

"Go home first thing in the morning, Jon. Think about what it means to love and serve Jesus, and then we'll talk toward the end of next week. I'll call you. Now go get some sleep."

"But Bruce!"

Bruce simply turned around and walked out, apparently not interested in anything else Jon had to say at 3:15 in the morning. Jon still stood there, stunned. *Man! This stinks! Everyone is going to think I'm an idiot! Mom is going to kill me… Now what, Lord? Do You care?*

Debriefing

WHAT DO YOU DO when you mess up?

Some people are deathly afraid to make mistakes. Perhaps they fear being made fun of, or letting people down, or even admitting to themselves that they aren't as good as they thought they were. Maybe they just have a hard time recovering from failures, and they just feel incredibly set back when they don't fulfill their own expectations.

One of the things I have loved about my own years of involvement at camp is that I have been allowed to mess up, learn from my mistakes, and move forward. I remember many of the gags I pulled at camp (yes, I even helped 'liberate' a podium in the middle of the night), getting caught, getting forgiven, learning some tough lessons, and moving on. Let me give you one example from my time as a cabin leader.

The Maple Mountain Man

Our camp had an old story that had been floating around in one form or another for years about the "Maple Mountain Man," a huge fella who lived up on the big forested hill next to the camp. As a camper, I don't know if I ever heard a well-developed story about him, just pieces and rumors, almost certainly 100% untrue. It had always intrigued me, so one summer I decided to develop the story and tell it to my campers.

The night came, darkness descended, and our cabin had no lights and open windows with canvas flaps. I began to weave a story about this man up on the hill who would come down and kidnap children he found. I kept it as vague as possible, telling them it was probably just rumors, and no one had ever proven his existence, but there were an awful lot of strange coincidences surrounding the stories. I don't remember all the details I gave, but I do remember the kids all sitting in the dark, on the wooden floor, away from the windows. They were completely into the story and doing a great job of scaring themselves and each other as I told the story.

I also arranged for a friend of mine, as the story progressed, to gently scrape the cabin with a stick from time to time, which further helped the campers get into the story. And then, the *coup de grace*: I had my friend dash into the pitch-black cabin, wearing red glowing eyes, look around, give a slight growl, and then run out again. That was it.

Of course, the campers were suitably terrified – and loved every minute of it! It worked better than I could possibly have hoped. Nobody wanted to sleep that night – or get back into their bunks by the windows. They were old enough to know it was just a story, and I was rather satisfied that they had enjoyed the experience, and I was proud of my success. My new version of the Maple Mountain Man would become famous in camp lore for years.

Technically, I hadn't broken any camp rules, though there probably should have been a rule against those kinds of stories, but that was in another day, and we got away with things like that at camp. However, I should have known better, and the next day, unbeknownst to me, my campers started telling other campers what had happened (or what they had perceived had happened), and soon we had kids crying all over the camp. I had an older cabin, and I think they knew deep down that it was all a joke, but the younger kids were terrified. Something had to be done, and I was called in to have a little chat with the director. It wasn't the first (or last) time.

That morning in chapel, I got up in front of everyone and admitted I had made up the whole story and there was no Maple Mountain Man. I apologized to all the campers, and things mostly calmed down after that.

I learned a lesson that day, not just about the harm of scary stories, but what it means to be a leader. I was proud, and I was careless. I began to realize that if I was going to be a good leader with good influence, I needed to start acting like it. Although I find it somewhat humorous now, I was quite humbled by the whole thing at the time, and I did learn and grow.

I'm very glad the director didn't simply send me home but showed me the grace I needed in that situation. However, if I had not learned from what I had done, and had I continued to do such things, I would have left him with no choice but to send me home.

Mistakes and Sins

When we mess up, we always have a choice of how we're going to respond to it. We can give up, or we can press on. But here's the thing: without good support around us, it is a lot harder to pick ourselves up each time. My experience with Christian camps has been that for every time I've done something really stupid – and there have been many, including ones much worse than described above – there has been someone there to help me see the poor choices I made, and someone who has helped me correct my ways, learn from the situation, and move on.

I do want to make one important distinction, however. As I mentioned in chapter six, there is a big difference between *sins* and *mistakes*. Jesus was sinless, but was He capable of cutting a board wrong or hitting His finger with a hammer? I think so. The difference between sins and mistakes is that sins are always first and foremost against God and His holy nature and decrees, whereas mistakes involve poor judgment and accidents. Sins involve acts of rebellion against God, either by what we do or fail to do; mistakes generally come from inexperience or carelessness. Sins are wrong moral choices; mistakes are poor choices that can be considered "amoral" or "not moral." Sins are "heart issues," whereas mistakes are often simply "head issues."

Why is this an important distinction? Primarily because when people mess up at camp, we need to try to determine if it was due to inexperience, carelessness, or moral failure. Most people get experience by making mistakes and being supported and moving on. Carelessness and moral failure, on the other hand, are much less simple. It is much easier to change your mind than to change your heart. Fortunately, we serve a God who is all about transforming hearts *and* minds.

In my blunder with the Maple Mountain Man story, it was not about a moral failing. I just didn't fully understand the ramifications of telling the story the way I did. I honestly thought I was being a great cabin leader and giving the kids a great experience. My eagerness for fun, combined with my inexperience, caused me to fail to think through the consequences. There were other times, however, when I knew the rules and chose to break them. Those were wrong moral decisions, and the consequences tended to be more severe, as they should have been.

I have heard people say, "It's never wrong if you learn from it!" This, of course, is foolishness. Although we need to learn from both our mistakes and our sins, doing so does not erase the nature of the sin or mistake. The good news is that God can take even our worst choices, our direst failings, and make good come of them.

What Do I Do Now?

So, when we mess up, what do we do? The first thing is to seek forgiveness from whomever we have hurt or offended. Even if we did not mean for it to happen, a good leader takes responsibility. Always. Even if it is mostly someone else's fault, we take ownership of what we did wrong. If it affected many people, you may need a public apology. If just a few, it can be a more private affair. It is good for us to be humbled from time to time, and how we respond in those times says a lot about our heart condition.

Second, it is often helpful to talk it through with someone who can help us get on the right track again. We will be talking about mentors later in the book, but for now, understand that in most cases, it is helpful to get feedback and accountability from someone who is more mature in the faith and possibly someone with more leadership experience.

Third, we need to accept and "own" the consequences of our actions. Sometimes that means we will lose privileges (like being grounded), or we will have to make it up in some way. My grade seven teacher often handed out 300-word essays when we disobeyed (which is where I learned many of my writing skills!). The worst thing we can do after messing up is to further rebel against the consequences. Choose to submit humbly, and you will show that you are truly repentant.

Finally, we need to seek God's power to help us move on. God never tempts us or causes us to sin, but when we do fall to temptation and then repent, He forgives us and uses those circumstances to teach us and to draw us closer to Him.

The Beauty of Brokenness

I have often taught a session to my leader trainees called, "The Broken Leader," where I show that the route from commitment to surrender is almost always brokenness. *Commitment* is trying to follow Jesus on our own strength, while *surrender* is submitting to God and admitting we can't do it without His strength.

The Apostle Peter is a great example of this when He constantly tried to follow Jesus. He even risked his life and walked on water with Jesus, and then he courageously stayed close by when Jesus was arrested. Yet no matter how hard he tried, he still messed up, to the point where he tried to dissuade Jesus from the cross and received the strongest rebuke possible – "Get behind me Satan!" – and to where he eventually denied Jesus three times. Peter was as *committed* to Jesus as humanly possible, but when the tough times came, he still messed up.

Imagine how broken Peter was from all this, and for days, it seemed like all his hopes and dreams had been destroyed. But Jesus came to Peter and restored him three times, once for every denial (see John 21:15-19). From that point on, although Peter still made mistakes, He never shrank back from following Jesus again. I believe his brokenness led to true *surrender* and a much deeper relationship with Jesus.

Contrast that with Judas, who betrayed Jesus and then went out and killed himself. Unwilling to be broken, he gave up before he could be forgiven and restored.

All of us come to times in our lives, especially as leaders, when we do something we deeply regret, and we can either give up, or we can learn from it, go deeper with Jesus, and move on. First John 1:9 says: "But if we confess our sins to him, he is faithful and just to forgive us our sins and to cleanse us from all wickedness."

What a joy it is to be forgiven! And not just forgiven, but *cleansed* of all the filth in our lives, all those things that keep us from being the people and the leaders God has called us to be.

Let us be the kinds of people who "fail forward," allowing our brokenness to lead us to the feet of Jesus for forgiveness and renewal. Let's be the kinds of leaders who recognize the need and place for grace when those around us fail. If people are willing to learn, change, and move on, we need to be their best supporters, especially as we remember our own failings.

Discussion Questions

1. Has your fear of failure ever kept you from trying something you later wished you had tried? How did you feel?

2. Have you ever been glad you attempted something and failed, simply because of what it taught you? If so, explain why.

3. What is the difference between a "sin" and a "mistake"? How do we recover from each?

4. What is the difference between "commitment" and "surrender"?

5. How can brokenness bring us into a deeper relationship with God?

6. Is there anything in your camp culture that needs to change so that people are free to "fail forward"? What can you do differently?

7. How do we love and correct one another (tough love) while leaving ample room for forgiveness and grace?

8. Is there brokenness in your life that God is using to draw you closer to Him? What areas of your life do you need to submit to Him more?

UNDERSTANDING &
PRESENTING THE GOSPEL

CHAPTER 11

When Everything Goes Wrong
Who is God?

MADISON SAT IN CHAPEL, barely hearing anything the speaker was saying. Her head hurt, and her stomach felt like something was trying to escape, its direction yet to be determined. *Why is it so stinking cold in here?! Oh, I feel awful. Please stop talking and let us go...*

The speaker wrapped up and began to pray, but Madison felt a sudden urge to throw up. She got up from her seat, ran out the back and found the bathroom just in time. Details of her next experiences are best left undescribed.

She thought she could hear Charlotte saying something in the background, but her brain was a complete fog. *Oh, no, here I go again...*

A day later, Madison was still in the infirmary, and she had plenty of company, as others had apparently caught the same bug. Some campers had been sent home, as well as a couple of the staff. Madison felt a little better but very weak and dehydrated.

"Think you can keep something down, Maddy?" asked Nurse Rose.

"Um, I dunno. Maybe some Jell-O or something?"

"Okay, let's try that and see how you feel."

It had been another tough week for Madison, even before getting sick. Her cabin group was better than last week, and she even felt like she was seeing them grow in faith, but nothing else seemed to be going right. Much of it could probably be chalked up to being overtired, but life, in general, seemed overwhelming. Even some of her friendships at camp, which had blossomed in the first few weeks, were now feeling strained. Every activity she led felt like a chore, and her quiet times in the mornings, which she had looked forward to in earlier weeks, were now almost non-existent. She felt like she had been in "survival mode" for about two weeks.

Adding to all this was the bad news she got from home. Her mom had recovered from cancer about seven years ago, but new tests were showing it was back. Madison wanted to go home and be with her, but her mom was adamant she stay at camp and stick it out for the summer.

"I'll be okay," she told Madison over the phone. "There will be plenty of time for you to worry about me when you're back in a couple of weeks."

Well, Lord? Anything else to throw at me? I'm as down as I can be, so You might as well hit me again.

Rose brought Madison some red Jell-O and set it beside her bed. "Would you like something to drink as well? I could get you an herbal tea or something?"

"No, thanks, I'm good. Let's see how I do with this, first."

"Okay, but let's not let you get any more dehydrated. You feeling any better?"

Madison hesitated briefly before answering, and tears began to form in her eyes. "I'm okay. A bit better, I guess."

Rose looked at her with eyes full of compassion. "But there's a lot more going on than just being sick, right?"

Madison looked down and began to sob gently. Rose reached over and gave her a gentle hug. "It's okay, sweetie. You want to talk about it?"

Madison took a few moments to pull herself together again and wipe her tears away. Then she nodded.

Rose pulled up a chair and sat down next to Madison's bed. "So, what's going on?" she asked gently. "Been a tough summer?"

"Yeah, it's been tough. I've learned tons, and I'm really glad to be here, but lately…" She shrugged. "It's been pretty awful. I really thought God loved me, but…" She looked down and shook her head.

"Of course He loves you, darling!"

"Well, if He loves me, and if He's good and mighty and all that, why does He always allow bad things to happen to me? I came here to serve Him, and things just keep getting worse." Madison went on to tell Rose about her mom and the cancer and so many other things weighing so heavily upon her.

Rose listened attentively, and Madison could tell she cared by her kind and gentle responses.

"I don't know, Rose. I just thought when you followed Jesus, He would make things better, not worse."

"I guess that depends on what you mean by *better*, doesn't it?"

Madison frowned. "What do you mean?"

"Well, there's the 'better' of God making everything perfect, which we won't see until heaven, but there's also the 'better' of a deeper relationship with Him. And sometimes He uses tough times to draw us closer to Him."

"But how does *afflicting* us make anything better?"

"Sometimes that's just the best way to get our attention. Pain has been called 'God's megaphone.' We can ignore all sorts of wooing from God, so-called blessings, prosperity, and so on, but pain and suffering are pretty hard to ignore."

"You're telling *me*. But *cancer*? How can God allow that and still be 'good'?"

"Maddy, honey, I can't answer that for this particular situation, but I've seen God take all sorts of evil and turn it around for His purposes. He doesn't *cause* evil, but He takes it and makes it work for His bigger purposes that we often simply can't see. And He promises to eradicate evil forever, in His perfect timing."

"But I just can't take any more of this! I just can't go through the cancer thing again with my mom!"

Rose's eyes were wet as she responded. "I know, sweetheart — *you* can't. But the God of compassion who lives in you *can*, and He'll bring you through. And I truly believe that one day it will all make sense, and we'll see how He used these things for good, and we'll worship Him for it. But it's so hard to see all that on this side of eternity."

Madison took a deep breath and then sighed. "I know you're right, but it's just so hard."

Rose gave her yet another hug. "Yes, it is. Jesus promised His followers that in this world they would see trouble, but then He said,

'Take heart! For I have overcome the world!' He's in control, and nothing escapes His notice or His control."

Madison gave something between a slight nod and a shrug, and Rose continued.

"Not only does He walk through the valleys with us and draw us closer to Him through these times, but He also takes those experiences and uses them in you to help others. I can sit here with you now because of the many valleys I've gone through. I know the pain you're feeling, and I'm not afraid to join you in it. Because *God* is my rock and my fortress, my help in time of trouble."

"Pray for me, Rose? Pray that I would see that and receive His comfort?"

"You bet. Lord, God, thank You that You love us so much that You walk through these dark valleys with us…"

"Hey, Mom, it's me."

"Jonny? What are you doing here?"

"Nice to see you, too, Mom." Jon pushed open the door and dropped his bags just inside. He saw his mom in the kitchen, standing with her hands on her hips, frowning at him.

"What's going on, Jonny? Why are you home in the middle of the week? I thought you were supposed to be there all summer." Her expression grew dark, and her eyes narrowed. "You didn't do something *stupid* again, did you?"

You mess up once, and you're labeled for life. "I don't really want to talk about it, Mom. Just some issues at camp. I'll be home for a bit and then go back in a week or so."

"You got booted out?! Well, that's what you get for hanging around a bunch of hypocrites." She shook her head and turned back to the sink where she had been rinsing some radishes.

"They're not hypocrites, Mom! Most of them are great. The director just doesn't have much of a sense of humor."

His mom turned back toward him, a sorrowful look on her face. "More practical jokes, Jon? I thought you would've learned your lesson when you were expelled from Bible School."

Jon felt his pulse race and his face redden. "Not *expelled*, Mom, just *suspended*. And *that* wasn't my fault, either."

"It's *never* your fault, Jon. When are you going to take responsibility for your life? If your dad were here, he'd give you a good —"

"Well, he's *not* here, is he, Mom? You made sure of that, didn't you?" That struck hard, and Jon immediately felt guilty for crossing a line.

"Now listen, I will *not* have you speaking to me like that! How could you possibly understand what happened between us? What do you know about it, anyway?"

Jon was in it now, and he wasn't backing down. "Oh, nothing, just heard hundreds of arguments, and you *belittling* him all the time! Maybe if you'd had a little grace, he would have stuck around!"

"Oh, you're one to talk about *grace*." She spat the word out like it was a poison. "One of your Christian words that means you do *whatever* you want and then you get *forgiven*. I know how that works, Jon. That's why you're in trouble all the time — you expect *grace* when you need *punishment* and *discipline*! What am I to do with you, Jonny? You're breaking my heart." In a matter of seconds, she had gone from anger to weeping. She brought her apron up to her eyes and dabbed them.

"Look, I'm sorry, Mom. Don't cry. I'm sorry. I just gotta figure things out for a bit." He wished he could hug his Mom, but those days were long past. His mom turned away and wiped her eyes some more. "I'll be up in my room."

Jon grabbed his bags and trudged up the stairs. Soon he was in his small room with the door closed. He looked around at his few things — an old-fashioned dresser, his well-used Fender guitar, a few books on a shelf, and a bedside table with a lamp. Things had been moved a little, so he knew his mom had been in here dusting and vacuuming. *I need to appreciate her more for all she does for me. Especially how she brought me up those years without Dad. I'm pretty fortunate to have somewhere to come home to.*

He sat on his bed and then flopped back to lie down. *Man! What am I doing here? I should be at camp where the action is. Thanks a lot, Bruce. Just ruin my summer.*

He turned his head and saw his Bible, sitting on the shelf, and he shook his head. *What's the point? That hasn't gotten me too far.*

But something inside him was telling him to read it, so after trying to ignore the feeling for almost twenty minutes, he sat up, leaned over, and pulled it out. He saw a bookmark in it and opened to Hebrews chapter 10. He began to read the chapter, and it was somewhat interesting, but when he reached verses 26 to 31, he started to get very uncomfortable. He read the verses over several times to make sure he was reading it correctly:

> Dear friends, if we deliberately continue sinning after we have received knowledge of the truth, there is no longer any sacrifice that will cover these sins. There is only the terrible expectation of God's judgment and the raging fire that will consume his enemies. For anyone who refused to obey the law of Moses was put to death without mercy on the testimony of two or three witnesses.
>
> Just think how much worse the punishment will be for those who have trampled on the Son of God, and have treated the blood of the covenant, which made us holy, as if it were common and unholy, and have insulted and disdained the Holy Spirit who brings God's mercy to us. For we know the one who said, "I will take revenge. I will pay them back." He also said, "The Lord will judge his own people." It is a terrible thing to fall into the hands of the living God.

Wow, have I ever read this before? He knew he'd read the book of Hebrews in Bible college, but he didn't remember ever reading these verses before. *Where's the grace? How can it speak of judgment when God is so loving? This doesn't make sense. I must be misreading it.*

He pulled out his phone, selected his Bible app, and proceeded to read the verses in a few other versions, but they all seemed to say the same thing. He then proceeded to read the verses in the context of the rest of the chapter and tried to remember who the book was being written to. *Jewish Christians. Believers. Does this mean I can lose my salvation?*

He knew from Bible college that some people believed that, but he had always maintained that "once saved, always saved" made the best sense of so many Scripture passages. Then again, he could also remember arguing that "eternal security" only applied to those who were *truly* saved.

Have I ever been truly saved? Am I one of these who is under judgment? Oh, God, please, no! Show me Your grace! Forgive me my many, many sins! Help me understand what it is You want from me!

He had a long, sleepless, and unhappy night ahead of him.

Jon looked up from his coffee to see Larry, the young adults' pastor from his church, coming in the door. He got up and shook Larry's hand. "Thanks so much for meeting with me, Larry. I really appreciate it."

Larry smiled wryly and said, "Well, you sounded pretty desperate when you called this morning at, what, 6:00?"

"Yeah, sorry, I couldn't wait any longer. I was awake most of the night. I haven't slept well since I got home." Dark circles under his eyes were good evidence of that. "Can I at least buy you a coffee or something?"

"Sure, that would be great. Black, please."

Jon went over to the counter, made the transaction, brought Larry his coffee, and sat down across from him.

They made small talk for a few minutes, and then Larry looked Jon in the eyes and said, "So, what's going on, Jon? You said on the phone you'd been asked to leave the camp for a while. And now you're having some kind of 'faith crisis,' I believe you called it?"

Jon cleared his throat. "Yeah, you could say that. Well, I guess I *did* say that, didn't I? It's – I just don't know where I stand with God. I've had a few pretty rough days since I came home, and I just wasn't sure what to do about it."

Larry continued to make eye contact, concern showing on his face. "So what's been going on?"

Jon looked down and carefully formed his words. "I'm not sure if I'm a Christian, anymore. I don't mean I've *lost* my salvation, but that maybe I never had it to begin with. I, I just don't think, I just, I don't know. It's complicated."

Larry nodded slowly. "Well, I can see why it's been a tough few days. Tell me this, Jon, what is a Christian?" he picked up his coffee and took a sip.

"Well, that's the thing. I thought I knew. I mean, at camp, it's easy. You're saved by faith in Jesus, who died and paid the penalty for our sins. But I just don't know if that is all there is to it. I mean, how many kids pray 'the prayer' and come back the next year completely unchanged? And how long have I been calling myself a Christian, but I still do all sorts of dumb things? The Bible says, 'Call on the name of Jesus, and you will be saved.' I did that. I really believed. But somehow, I think a Christian has to be someone who is really following Jesus. Like 100%. I'm at about 10%. So, I really don't know if I'm saved yet. I think there's something missing, like I haven't done enough, or maybe not the right things."

Larry warmed his hands on his coffee and thought for a moment. "That's the thing, isn't it, Jon? If it's by works, we can never be sure we're saved. When have we done enough? When are we following Jesus closely enough?"

"Exactly. So, yeah, I know it's by God grace, through faith, but 'faith without works is dead,' right? And I'm afraid, like I was reading in Hebrews 10, that I've trampled God's grace, that I've kept on sinning after receiving the truth. I've always relied on the fact that God is *love*, but as I've been reading the last few days, I'm beginning to think maybe God is also a Judge, and I'm in big trouble."

Larry nodded again. "I think that's where we often go wrong, Jon. We tend to either emphasize God's *love*, or we emphasize His *holiness*, while ignoring the other. God is *both*, and He's a whole lot more than that. We have to stop putting Him in a box."

Larry straightened in his chair and continued. "When we ignore His holiness, we tend to think we can do whatever we want and receive forgiveness. Paul says to that, in Romans 6:1-2, 'Well then, should we keep on sinning so that God can show us more and more of his wonderful grace? Of course not! Since we have died to sin, how can we continue to live in it?'"

Jon shook his head miserably. "That's what I've been doing, Larry. I'm totally messed up."

"*But*," Larry emphasized, "Paul says just two chapters later in Romans 8:1, 'So now there is no condemnation for those who belong to Christ Jesus.' So, if we are truly believers, then we cannot be condemned." Larry pulled a small, worn Bible out of his pocket and flipped the pages. "And look what it says at the end of Hebrews 10, the passage you were talking about: 'But *we* do not belong to those who shrink back and are destroyed, but to those who have faith and are *saved.*' The writer of Hebrews said, yeah, don't trample God's grace, but to the Christians he was writing to, he also said – that's not you guys! You were saved by faith!"

Jon looked down at his coffee and said nothing. *It's not that simple...*

"I'm saying that you're right, you can't ignore God's holiness, but you can't ignore His love and grace, either. When we forget about how loving God is, we go back to trying to *earn* our salvation. We start inventing and obeying man-made rules, like what you can and can't do on Sundays. But by keeping the proper tension between God's love and holiness, we realize that God hates sin and rebellion, but when we sin, He's always ready to forgive us and help us move on. He knows our frailty."

"So that it?" Jon asked. "Just ask forgiveness and move on? I've done that. I screw up, I ask forgiveness, I screw up, I ask forgiveness, I screw up... Larry what I really want is to stop screwing up!" Jon could feel a tear forming in the side of his eye.

"Jon, let me ask you something. What's your prayer life like?"

Jon didn't look up, and he didn't say anything for a while. Then he looked Larry in the eyes and said, "Not very good."

"And how often do you read the Bible when you aren't doing it for a course or assignment?"

Jon shrugged. "Not much. But are you saying that's my problem? Not having regular 'devotions'? Sounds like *legalism* to me, just like you were warning against."

Larry gave a wry chuckle. "Doing what is *right* is never legalism. Legalism is adding laws that God – our legitimate authority over us – never gave us. I've heard people say that driving the speed limit is legalistic. Actually, no, it's just obeying the law! But on the other hand, if you were to insist that everybody you knew had to drive 5 kilometers *under* the speed limit, just to make sure they never went over it, well, that would be legalism."

"Yeah, I guess."

"Regular time in the Word and in prayer could become legalistic if you think that those practices will save you, but if you *are* saved, they are wonderful practices, among others, that will help you stay on track with God."

Jon nodded. *Maybe.*

Larry continued. "The reason I'm asking about your devotional life is not because there's a formula that will make you holy. But these spiritual disciplines, like studying God's Word, praying, fasting, giving, and so on, well, these have been used for centuries by believers who loved God and desired to be close to Him. They are often very good indications of where our hearts are."

Jon nodded again. "Fair enough."

"In fact, show me a believer's day-timer and his credit card statement, and I could pretty much, 99% of the time, tell you where his heart is at. What you do with your so-called 'free-time' and how you spend your money are almost always true tests of your spiritual life."

"So, I just need to work harder? Try harder?" *I've tried that before!*

Larry shook his head violently. "No, no! That's *not* what I'm saying! I'm saying you need to love God more than you love yourself."

Jon looked confused. "But I *don't* love myself. I'm a jerk."

"Of course, you do. You may not 'feel good' about yourself, but most of what you do is for *you*, and most of what you think about is *you*. Right?"

Jon nodded grimly.

"*Love* in the Bible is always to do with *actions*, not feelings. Jesus said that if we love Him, we'll obey His commands. He's not saying that we'll just feel good feelings toward Him, though those will also come as we obey Him and draw closer to Him."

Larry picked up his coffee mug and gazed into it thoughtfully. "No, we love ourselves far too much. That's why Jesus said that the second greatest command, after loving God, was to love our neighbors as *ourselves*. Show concern for others as we regularly do for ourselves."

"But how do I love God and others more? I stink at this." *I really do. I'm hopeless!*

"We all do, Jon. That's why we need the Holy Spirit to transform our lives. The spiritual disciplines, when used to pursue God, open us up to His moving in our lives. They are a form of surrender to Him. Sometimes God has to break us before we will surrender to Him. Kind of like working with a wild horse. That horse only becomes truly useful when it will settle down and obey its master."

A small smile crept onto Jon's face. "Yeah, I guess I've been a bit of a wild horse."

Larry nodded and took a sip of coffee. "Jon, it's the thirsty man who desperately looks for water; it's the sick man who seeks a doctor. God promises that if we truly seek Him, we'll find Him. When you are ready, He's there."

Jon sat up a bit, leaned forward, and put his hands on the table. "So, you're saying there's no simple answer, then. Seek God with all my heart, surrender to His will, and He'll begin to change me. And things like prayer and studying the Word are ways to seek after God and surrender to Him. Is that what you're saying?"

Larry nodded and gave an encouraging grin. "Yeah, I think that's a pretty good summary. There are no easy answers, no formulas for success, but there are biblical principles to apply to our lives. Seek God and obey what you know to be His will. If you're in His Word and in prayer, His will becomes extremely obvious for the vast majority of our decisions."

Jon was nodding but seemed to be deep in thought.

"And one more thing, Jon, do it in *community*. Don't try to be a lone ranger. You need people who you can trust, who you can be accountable to, and who will be accountable to you, people who will pray for you and with you and hold you up when you stumble and call you out when you stray."

Jon looked at Larry nervously. "Will you do that for me? Can you help me be accountable?"

Larry thought carefully before answering. "Sure, Jon, as long as you're buying the coffee! But seriously, I'll help you if you promise to be real and listen to my advice. I'll pray for you, too, but I'm not going to be easy on you. You need to get back to the Word and prayer and maybe a few other things we'll talk about." Larry pulled out his phone and looked at his calendar. "Let's meet again in two days, right here, at say 6:30?"

"I usually have supper around then."

"No, I mean in the *morning*! I have a full day, but we can get together and pray and talk about what God's been showing us the last couple of days. Sound good?"

"Six-thirty, *a.m.? Seriously?*" Jon thought for a moment. "Okay fine. But don't expect me to be awake."

"That's what the coffee's for. In the meantime, I'd like you to read the Gospel of John."

"In just *two* days?"

"Yes, in *two* days! You've got nothing better to do. And spend some time in prayer, too."

"Okay, Larry. It's a deal. Can we, uh, pray before we go? I really could use it…"

"Of course. Father God, we love you and ask that you would help Jon…"

Debriefing

I THINK MOST OF US hit a crisis of faith at one time or another. I certainly have more than once. It usually comes down to two things: what we believe about God and what we believe about ourselves. The first step is to firmly understand that we are not God!

God has many attributes that make up His revealed nature, and most of them are themes that we see repeated many times in the Bible. We are taught that God is loving, eternal, holy, just, good, faithful, all-powerful, omnipresent, all-knowing, and wise. These are fundamental and fairly easy to understand, though no list of attributes can truly define Him. We also know that He is relational, unified in Himself, yet made up of three equal, distinct, and fully God Persons: the Father, the Son, and the Holy Spirit.

As for us, we are created by God, made in His image, yet finite in our knowledge, power, wisdom, and so on. Our life comes from Him, and apart from Him sustaining us, we could not exist. Due to our sinful nature and the sins we commit, the image of God in us is corrupted, as is all of Creation. And due to that corruption, we begin life in a state of death and dying, both physically and spiritually. We are spiritually separated from God, and our bodies decay from birth until our physical death. In the next chapter, we will be looking at how trusting in Jesus changes all of that.

God has created us in His image, but in our sinful state, we try to remake Him in *our* image, making Him into something we can understand and relate to apart from His revealed Word. So, we decide that He is a "force," not a person, or that He is "nature," rather than the separate creator of nature, or that He is just one of us, and we, too, are gods or becoming part of God.

Even many who claim to follow Jesus do this, making statements like, "Well, *my* God would never allow babies to suffer." First of all, God doesn't belong to you, and second, how about we read His Word and find out what *He* says about suffering?! It is arrogant to determine who and what God is apart from His revealed Word.

Our sin nature, left unchecked, causes us to rebel against God's will, when what we need is to submit our will to His. Proverbs 1:7 tells us:

> Fear of the Lord is the foundation of true knowledge, but fools despise wisdom and discipline.

Until we acknowledge that God's wisdom is higher than ours, until we submit to His wisdom and instruction, we will always have an inaccurate view of God. And we will make treasonous declarations as to Who He is and how He acts in this world.

Goodness, Love, & Holiness

I think the most common attributes of God that Christians deny, whether purposefully or not, are God's goodness, His love, or His holiness. When we deny His goodness or His love, we begin to believe that God does not have the best for us at heart. We may see a relationship with God as a bunch of rules to follow, and we may become legalistic.

But when we deny His holiness, which I think today is much more common, we tend to downplay the need to obey God and follow Him. Life can become a series of compromises because we live like forgiveness is cheap and readily available, forgetting the price Jesus paid for it. We may even begin to deny the reality of hell or punishment, and we may wonder why our Christian lives have become so ineffective.

I believe the only antidote to these errors is to "be transformed by the renewing of our minds" (Romans 12:2). This requires a steady diet of

God's Word and choosing daily to obey it, submitting to the leading of His Spirit.

If we want to be effective and productive in leadership or any kind of ministry, it is essential that we get to know the God we serve and grow in our faith. Look at 2 Peter 1:5b-8:

> Supplement your faith with a generous provision of moral excellence, and moral excellence with knowledge, and knowledge with self-control, and self-control with patient endurance, and patient endurance with godliness, and godliness with brotherly affection, and brotherly affection with love for everyone. The more you grow like this, the more productive and useful you will be in your knowledge of our Lord Jesus Christ.

You will become like whoever you spend the most time with, so make sure that Person is Jesus!

Discussion Questions

1. Have you ever wondered if you were truly a Christian, especially after you messed up (again)?

2. Which do you see God more like: a loving Father who always wants the best for you or a righteous King who expects you to obey?

3. What do you think happens in our minds when we deny the love of God? How do we act?

4. Do you think there is anything you can do to make God love you more or less than He does right now? If so, what? If not, why not?

5. What do you think happens in our minds when we deny the holiness of God? How do we act?

6. What do you think it means that we are to "fear God"? See Luke 12:4-5.

7. What do you think happens in our minds when we deny the goodness of God? How do we act?

8. If God is good and loving, why do you suppose He allows Christians to suffer?

CHAPTER 12

Broken People, Hope-Filled Hearts
The Christian Life

THE BREEZE WAS LIGHT, the morning was fresh, and the low sun filtered through the leaves of the trees. Birds twittered joyously, and Madison breathed deeply as she walked. *I may never be a morning person, but this is glorious. Thank you, Lord!*

Beside her, Jessica's steps fell lightly onto the path, barely making a sound. She was a tiny thing for thirteen years old, though she made up for it by being loud and boisterous most of the time. Today, however, she was deep in thought.

It was her sobs that had woken Madison in the middle of the night, and it was all Madison could do to console Jessica and help her get back to sleep, with the promise of a chat in the morning. Madison made sure they stayed within view of the main camp buildings, as she did not want to be "alone" anywhere with a camper. But this at least gave them the opportunity to speak privately.

"So, Jess," Madison began. "What's going on?"

Their walk continued in silence as Jessica tried to get her thoughts together. Finally, she spoke. "Well, you know I don't come from a Christian family, right?"

"Yeah. Actually, most kids here don't."

"Really? Oh, I thought everyone just kinda knew about all this Jesus stuff."

Madison laughed softly. "Well, no, not really. A few may attend a local church, but most of the campers have pretty much learned about Jesus right here. Of course, lots of them come back year after year, so they get to know the songs, and they may remember some of what is taught. But believe me, you're not alone in not having grown up with this stuff. I didn't either."

They continued to walk along silently for a stretch. "I guess you're wondering why I was so upset last night?"

"It happens to all of us, Jess. I cry at night sometimes, too."

Jessica looked up at her with surprise. "Yeah, well, it just kind of hit me last night when the speaker was talking about how Jesus paid for all my sins by dying on the cross, and well, that's supposed to be good news, right?"

"Yes, it *is* good news. Isn't it?"

"Well, yeah, I guess, but then I was thinking about all that I've done wrong… There's a lot of stuff, Maddy!" Jessica's eyes began to tear up. There was bench close by, along the path, so Madison indicated for them to have a seat.

"But that's why Jesus died, Jess. Because there's too much *stuff*, too much sin, too much brokenness, too much pain for us to overcome on our own. Jesus' death on the cross means that we don't have to die; we don't have to try to pay the price."

Jessica looked up at Madison. "But that's what I'm afraid of. I thought God loved everybody, but now I'm realizing that He doesn't love those who don't love Him!"

Madison's heart was breaking for this young girl. "Jess, He loves *everyone*, more than we could ever understand, and He offers eternal life to anyone who calls on His name, who puts their trust in Him, no matter what we've done!"

"But that's the trouble, Maddy! He demands that we trust in Him, and if we don't, then He's going to punish us! Forever!"

Oh, that's what she's getting at. Hell. Eternal punishment. "But Jess, you sound like you believe, which means that God is rescuing you from all that. All you have to do is trust in Jesus, who He is and what He did on the cross for you, and you will have eternal life! You will be one of His children forever!"

Jessica didn't say anything. Her head dropped down, and she sobbed quietly. Madison put her arm around her gently.

"Jessica, are you ready to receive God's free gift of salvation? Do you want to pray and tell God about it?"

Jessica's breathing became more rapid, and then she looked up, tears in her eyes, and exclaimed, "It's not that simple, Maddy!"

"But it is, sweetheart. God's gift of eternal life is available to anyone who turns from their sins and turns to God, believing in Jesus. It doesn't matter what you've done, where you've been, who you think you are, or any of those things. It's just a small step of faith that says, 'God, I know I'm a sinner, that I've rebelled against You and failed to keep Your perfect law. But I believe that Jesus died for me, paying for my sin on that cross, and then He rose from the dead, conquering death and bringing eternal life to all who put their trust in You. And so today, I do that. I want to be one of Your children.'"

Jessica sighed and shook her head. "Maddy, I get all that, I really do, and I believe it's true. But I just can't become a Christian!"

"Why not, Sweetie?"

'Because… I'll be leaving my parents behind, and they'll go to *hell*!" Jessica burst into tears once again and buried her head on Madison's shoulder.

Light suddenly dawned in Madison's head, and it finally began to make sense to her. "Oh, oh, Jess, I'm so sorry I just didn't get what was bothering you. I see what you're saying." She gave Jessica a little squeeze as the tears continued to pour out.

I should have seen that coming! Lord, now what? She's right, she'll be leaving her parents behind. What do I tell her? Madison waited for a reply. *The truth? Of course, always the truth, but what aspect of it? Just the truth?*

"Jessica, there's no point denying what you said is true. It is possible that if you give your life to Jesus, your parents won't understand and won't receive Him as well. And if they choose to ignore God for the rest of their lives, yes, the Bible tells us they will be eternally separated from Him. But does that mean that you can just turn away from what you know to be true?"

Jessica wiped her eyes and stared off back toward the Dining Hall. She remained silent for a while longer, obviously pondering, then spoke softly. "It just doesn't seem fair. They're good people, Maddy, even if they don't know about Jesus."

"From what you've told me, I'm sure they're wonderful parents, Jessica. But." She paused and thought for a moment. "But Jess, are any of us actually *good*, in God's eyes? Like sinless?"

"Well, no, I guess not. We've all messed up, right? I mean, some people might be good compared to others, but not compared to Jesus or compared to God's laws, right?"

Wow, this one learns fast. "Exactly, Jess. You've been paying attention..."

A small smile came and then faded quickly on Jessica's face.

"But, Jess, you've forgotten one really important thing."

"What's that?"

"What did Pastor Joel say we're supposed to do with good news?"

"Share it?"

"Yeah. Share it. Like he said, if you had the cure for cancer, and someone you loved had cancer, you wouldn't keep that from them, would you?"

"No, I guess not. But what if they don't believe? What if I become a Christian, and I tell my parents, and they just laugh at me? What then?"

"Well, then you pray and *keep* praying until God gets hold of their hearts and changes them."

"And what if He doesn't?"

"But what if He does? Jess, we can't see the future, and it's not our job to know what is going to happen or to worry about any of that. All we can do is obey God, which includes telling others the good news, and then let Him be God and do His thing in people's hearts. Maybe God wants to use you to help rescue your parents."

Jess looked like she was going to say something but then changed her mind.

Madison plowed ahead. "You're right, Jess, there's no guarantee that they will believe. But your first responsibility is to decide for *yourself* if this all makes sense and if you want to follow Jesus. Not only do we have to put our faith in Jesus to *become* a Christian, but the life of a Christian continues, right up until we see Him face to face, it continues by *faith*. As a Christian, I constantly have to trust God for *everything*."

"But that's easy for you."

"What?!" Madison almost laughed. "Easy? For *me*?! Oh, Jessica, you have no idea the struggles I have daily! Being a camp cabin leader this summer has been the hardest thing I've ever done! Most of the time, I feel like I have no idea what I'm doing, and some of the time this summer I've felt like a complete failure! It's only my trust in God that keeps me here – or got me here in the first place!"

Jessica's brow furrowed. "But I thought being a Christian meant everything got *easier*."

Madison paused and thought for a moment. "No, not easier. Better, for sure, but not easier. Following Jesus is hard. He takes you places that you would never have chosen on your own. And the enemy is constantly trying to take you down. Jesus even promised His followers that they would certainly have trouble in this world, but you know what He said next?"

Jessica shrugged her shoulders.

"He said, 'Take heart! For I have overcome the world!' A wise lady reminded me of that verse when I needed it badly, not so long ago. You see, Jesus doesn't promise that our troubles will go away, but He does promise to be *with* us through our troubles, through our trials."

"So that's the advantage of being a Christian?"

"Sorry?"

"Well, you're saying that we're going to have problems either way, but Christians at least get Jesus to help them through them, right?"

Madison nodded. "Yeah, I think that's a good way to look at it. And then there's the whole heaven and eternity with Jesus thing."

Jessica sighed. "Yeah, or without Him if you don't believe. Maddy, I think I know what I need to do, but I'm just so afraid for my parents. Can you please pray for me?"

"Of course. Let's do that…"

The morning was young, and the coffee hadn't quite taken effect yet. Larry looked wide awake as he sipped on his hot chocolate, but Jon was still feeling the effects of another late night.

Larry looked at Jon and said, "So. Back to camp tomorrow, I hear?"

Jon nodded and took another sip of his coffee. This was the fourth time in a week and a half they'd met at this coffee shop. It had good coffee, nice servers, *amazing* cinnamon buns, and a terrible name: "Bean Awesome." *Well, I guess three out of four ain't bad.*

Larry asked, "How did your meeting with Bruce go?"

Jon gave a short laugh. "Thanks to you, pretty well. He seems to think I put you up to it, though."

"Well, you kind of did, but I was happy to let him know we've been meeting and that you've been working hard to change and grow this last bit. I told him I thought you were ready to come back. And this way, I don't have to keep meeting with you every few days." Larry smiled at his jest.

"Well, I really do appreciate it, Larry. Thanks. It's funny, I don't think I realized the influence I was having on everyone at camp until all this happened, but it's been a good chance to reflect on where I'm at in life and where I want to be in the next few years. Actually, it was something you said last time that really affected me."

"Do tell."

"Remember when we were talking about my leadership style and how I tend to lead with strong authority but little grace?"

"Yeah."

"And you said that ministry is all about *people*, not *programs*?"

"Sure."

"Well, it wasn't really new to me, but it suddenly made sense. You know what I mean?"

"I think so, but keep going." Larry wiped some hot chocolate fuzz from his mustache with the back of his hand.

"Yeah, well, I was thinking about my purpose in life, and what it means to be a Christian. I mean, I've pretty much been a Christian since I was four years old, and I guess I've had it pretty easy in a lot of ways. I'm good at most things I do, people generally like me, and I've never struggled in school."

"Straight A's, I think you told me."

"Yeah, and to be honest, I found school pretty easy. In fact, if it was hard, I probably would've given up and failed. Apart from my family, which has been a bit of a disaster, I've had all the advantages, not to mention a great church and, of course, salvation itself."

"Those are pretty important, too."

"Exactly. And so, I've been able to coast, to be the funny guy in class, to be popular, and all that stuff. But my character hasn't exactly been the best. I've disappointed God – and a lot of people, too."

Larry said nothing, but he nodded.

"And I think being a Christian is a lot more than just going through the motions. It's loving God with everything we have in us, and then, with His love in us, loving everyone we come into contact with. I haven't done that. It's been a big game for me to try to impress people. It hasn't been about serving God, even at camp, but about *me* and what I can get out of it. I don't think that's been very pleasing to God."

Larry nodded again. "So now what?"

"I gotta make some changes! Well, I mean God needs to change me. I honestly feel like I've just woken up to what life is all about, and I'm excited to get back to camp and serve Him."

Larry looked at Jon and cautioned him, "It's not going to be easy, Jon, because people at camp think they know what you're like, and they're going to expect more of the same. What will you do differently?"

Jon thought for a moment and replied, "I don't know, but things are going to have to change. Any ideas?"

"Well, for starters, do you think there are some people you should apologize to?"

Jon looked down for a second and then looked up at Larry again. "Yeah, quite a few, probably. That's not going to be easy…"

Larry nodded. "No, it won't. What else do you think you need to do?

"Well, like we talked about earlier, I need to have accountability, someone who will tell me when I'm being a jerk. And, like you've been insisting, I need to keep myself in God's Word, not just to teach it to the kids, but for *me*, to develop my relationship with God. And I really want to make prayer more of a thing in my life. Like every day, get up early to pray and read God's Word."

"You? Early?" Larry raised an eyebrow.

"Yeah, me. Early! With coffee, of course. But I gotta do this! I know I'm a huge influence, and that means my relationship with God is going to affect everyone around me. I can only be effective to the degree that God is working in me and through me! I gotta seek Him with my whole heart!"

"Sounds like you really are ready to go back to camp, Jon. And I'm so glad that Bruce is willing to give you another chance. But, yeah, remember why you're there. You're responsible to Bruce, but you're serving Jesus Christ, and there is no higher calling. It all depends on you being connected to Jesus. Do you remember what it said in John's Gospel about being connected to Jesus, the True Vine?"

Jon responded excitedly. "Absolutely! It said that apart from Jesus, we can do nothing. *Nothing.* I get that now. Ministry is being connected to Him, surrendered to His Spirit, and then pouring out His love on everyone we meet. At camp, that means loving the campers and also the staff. I really want to do that."

"So, who's going to keep your feet to the fire? Who are you going to be accountable to?"

"Well, I'm thinking of asking Bruce, believe it or not. I think it should probably be a guy, and, well, yeah."

"I think that's a great choice. Bruce may be getting on in years now, and sure, he's a little fussy about certain things, but he's a solid man of God, and I know he truly cares about you. Even if he does get a little annoyed with your shenanigans." Larry raised an eyebrow quizzically.

Jon stifled a laugh. "Well, he won't have to worry. Not much anyway. I mean, I might still do a few funny things here and there, but I'll be *mostly* good."

"I think if you want to be effective, you should probably ask Bruce's permission before pulling off *any* pranks, Jon. Isn't that the camp policy anyway?"

"Well, something like that. I'll be good, *really*! I just don't want to be boring. So, yeah, I guess I'll have to trust Bruce's judgment if I want to let him keep me accountable." He thought for a moment. "Man! That's going to be tough!"

"Just remember *who* it's all for, Jon. Two weeks of camp left. Not too many opportunities left to make a difference in lives."

Jon paused, then nodded. "You're right, of course. It's so easy to get side-tracked by things that are fun but meaningless in the big picture. Thanks for the reminder."

"How's your mom doing?"

"Ah, she's okay. We had a surprisingly good chat yesterday, no, the day before. I apologized for the way I had spoken to her, especially about my dad, and she began to tell me a bit about how hard it had been raising me as a single mom these past few years. I still feel terrible about my witness to her. It's no wonder she doesn't believe."

Larry turned his head and looked out the window. Then he held his empty mug and examined it. "I'm not sure what to tell you, Jon, but I'm glad you guys were able to talk. The trouble is, we can fake it around other people, but usually, our family and close friends know when we're not sincere about something. There's no going back, but you can pray for her and start to live out your faith more consistently in front of her. God will do the rest."

"Yeah, I do pray for her, or at least I've started to this past week. I just feel like such a hypocrite trying to tell her about Jesus when she's seen what I've been like. I guess that's why character matters so much, hey? But God is changing me, so there's hope, right?"

"Where there's God, there's always hope, my friend. And just remember that your character won't change overnight. Character is developed bit by bit, little decision by little decision. Just walk with God, day by day, and He'll take care of changing you. And I think your mom will notice the change, too."

"Thanks, Larry. I really appreciate your time and your help."

Larry grinned. "That's my job, but also my joy, Jon. To point people to the Savior. Even at," he looked at his watch, "6:55 in the morning."

"Don't remind me, Larry!" The coffee had begun to do its job, but it was still *way* too early, especially on a day off from camp.

Debriefing

I THINK THERE ARE a lot of people like Jon, calling themselves Christians but not living it out, saying they serve God, but in fact serving themselves. Maybe you're one of those people? I've been there.

It's easy to think we're Christians because we grew up with Christian parents, or grew up in a supposedly Christian country. Or maybe we go to church regularly, so we think that counts for something. Maybe we made some kind of commitment years ago that we believed was "fire insurance" against an eternity in hell. Or maybe we generally follow the teachings of Jesus or know a lot about the Bible.

But none of those things will save you. A Christian is not only saved *from* the penalty of their sins by the finished work of Jesus on the cross, but they are saved *to* eternal life in Him, a transformed life, starting now. And we know that this can only occur through *faith* in Jesus. Ephesians 2:8-9 says:

> God saved you by his grace when you believed. And you can't take credit for this; it is a gift from God. Salvation is not a reward for the good things we have done, so none of us can boast about it.

As we've discussed, that's where the Christian life begins. It begins through faith in Jesus, based on the grace (undeserved favor) of God in sending Jesus to die in our place. But that's not the end. The very next verse says this:

> For we are God's masterpiece. He has created us anew in Christ Jesus, so we can do the good things he planned for us long ago.

Before you were born, God already knew you and loved you and had incredible plans for your life that only you could fulfill by trusting in Him and living for Him. God doesn't want any of us simply to say a prayer and then walk away. What begins by faith must continue in faith. As God says in Hebrews 11:6:

> And it is impossible to please God without faith. Anyone who wants to come to him must believe that God exists and that he rewards those who sincerely seek him.

And He tells us in Romans 1:17:

> This Good News tells us how God makes us right in his sight. This is accomplished from start to finish by faith. As the Scriptures say, "It is through faith that a righteous person has life."

Being a Christian isn't simply a one-time decision, but a life of faith and faithfulness, "from start to finish."

Being a Disciple

Acts 11:26 tells us the first use of the name "Christian." Apparently, it was a derogatory term used by their enemies, literally meaning "little Christs." The passage says, "The disciples were called Christians first at Antioch." Who were called Christians? The *disciples*.

So, what is a disciple? Imagine if I decided to call myself a disciple of a famous soccer player like Cristiano Ronaldo. What would be required for me to be considered his disciple?

Well, first, I would have to *play* soccer. A *lot*. Not just talk about soccer. I would need to study his style of soccer and learn to imitate the way he plays. I would try to get as close to him as I could and be coached by him if possible. I would attend his games and take an interest in everything he did so that I could become like him. I might even try to style my hair the same way and wear the same kinds of clothes he wears. Everything I did would be to try to become like him in every way possible. And, hopefully, people would look at me and say, "Wow, that Cristiano Ronaldo must be amazing!"

If we are true Christians, "little Christs," disciples of Jesus, these same principles must apply. Everything we put our efforts would be about Him and for His glory, not our own. W would not merely read about Him or quote His words, but get close to Him and love what He loves (i.e. people) and hate what He hates (i.e. sin and self-righteousness). We would become like Him in our compassion for the poor and needy, and we would talk about Him to everyone we meet. We would tell others how amazing it is to serve Him and to be saved by Him. We would learn to forgive as He has forgiven us.

Do people look at you and exclaim, "Wow, Jesus must be amazing!"?

Having the Right Purpose and Goals

The whole idea of a disciple is one who is *disciplined*. That's a bad word today, except maybe for athletes. But why is it that an athlete is so disciplined? Why do they work hour after hour, day after day, for years, trying to get to the absolute pinnacle of fitness and ability in their sport? They must have one goal, to be the best they can possibly be and thereby *win*. And yet it's all for earthly fame and maybe riches.

But as Christians, we are told in Matthew 6:19-21:

> Don't store up treasures here on earth, where moths eat them and rust destroys them, and where thieves break in and steal. Store your treasures in heaven, where moths and rust cannot destroy, and thieves do not break in and steal. Wherever your treasure is, there the desires of your heart will also be.

And in 1 Corinthians 9:24-25, God tells us:

> Don't you realize that in a race everyone runs, but only one person gets the prize? So run to win! All athletes are disciplined in their training. They do it to win a prize that will fade away, but we do it for an eternal prize.

A Christian is one who has been saved by faith but continues to run, no matter how hard it gets, no matter what happens, looking toward the prize of eternal life in Jesus. Each of us is to bear a cross, as Jesus told His disciples in Matthew 16:24-27:

> If any of you wants to be my follower, you must give up your own way, take up your cross, and follow me. If you try to hang on to your life, you will lose it. But if you give up your life for my sake, you will save it. And what do you benefit if you gain the whole world but lose your own soul? Is anything worth more than your soul? For the Son of Man will come with his angels in the glory of his Father and will judge all people according to their deeds.

Being a Christian isn't easy. We're promised hardships, but we're also promised the presence of Jesus through it all. Look at Jesus' Great Commission to His disciples, the final words in Matthew (28:18-20):

> I have been given all authority in heaven and on earth. Therefore, go and make disciples of all the nations, baptizing them in the name of the Father and the Son and the Holy Spirit. Teach these new disciples to obey all the commands I have given you. *And be sure of this: I am with you always, even to the end of the age* (emphasis mine).

As a Christian, as a disciple of Jesus, it is my calling and privilege to live and, if necessary, to die for Him. Yet the greatest gift of all is His presence, His Holy Spirit in our lives, right up until the day we meet Him face to face. I am not a Christian because of any works I have done, am doing, or plan to do. But because He has saved me from death, I have crossed over to life (John 5:24), and it is my joy to serve Him forever.

Discussion Questions

1. How would you define the word "Christian"? How do you know if you truly are a Christian?

2. Why do you think so many people believe that they are required to "work" their way to God?

3. How does a person become a Christian?

4. If works don't save us, what place do works have in our Christian lives?

5. Do people look at you and say, "Wow, that Jesus must be amazing!"? Why or why not?

6. How can you live in a way to store up treasure in heaven?

7. What do you think it means to deny yourself, take up your cross, and follow Jesus? Why does it matter that we do that?

CHAPTER 13

Greased Toilets & Being Born Young
Sharing a Testimony

H EY, CHARLOTTE!"
Charlotte turned and looked up from her desk, her face unreadable. "Oh, hi, Jon. So, you're back, hey?"

"Yeah, Bruce decided to give me another chance."

Charlotte nodded, keeping her expression neutral.

"Look, Charlotte, I – look I'm sorry I've been difficult to work with this summer. I just, well, I'm not even going to try to explain away my behavior. I've been wrong, and this last week or so has given me a lot of opportunities to think about my life and the way I've been acting. Anyway, I just want to say I'm sorry, okay?"

Charlotte's eyebrows lifted. "Really? You're not just saying that?"

Jon grimaced a little and sat down opposite Charlotte. "You don't mind if I sit?"

Charlotte shrugged. "Go for it. I'm expecting Madison any minute."

"Sure, I won't take much of your time, but I –"

Just then Madison walked in, looked at Jon and said, "Oh, sorry to interrupt. I can come back…"

"No, no," Jon said. "I won't be long." He stood up. "Here, have a seat." Madison hesitated, looked and Charlotte who shrugged and nodded, and then sat in the seat Jon had just vacated.

"Listen, you both might as well hear this. I was just going to say that this past week off has been really eye-opening for me. I've spent a lot of time thinking and praying, reading the Bible, and meeting with my pastor, and I can see that I've been a real jerk this summer – maybe my whole life."

A wry smile came onto Charlotte's face. "Well, I don't know about your whole life, but you have been rather difficult to deal with this summer."

"I know, and that's why I wanted to apologize. You see, I've been really arrogant, and I've been bringing shame to the name of Jesus. I realized while I was at home that it's not good enough to just be saved, but God wants us to live for Him *all* the time. Real faith in Him has to result in godly living, or we have to question whether or not we were saved in the first place."

Jon paused, and Charlotte jumped in. "Well, no one's perfect, Jon, but I do agree one hundred percent that our *walk* has to match our *talk*." Charlotte tilted her head at an angle, curious. "So, what happened, Jon? I've never heard you talk like this."

Jon smiled widely, his perfect teeth showing, and the girls both remembered why he was so popular. "What happened? I don't really know! All I can say, like the blind man Jesus healed, is that once I was blind, but now I see! Seriously, I feel giddy, the newness that I'm experiencing!"

No one interrupted him, so he continued. "For years, I admit it, I've lived trying to impress people, trying to somehow make *me* feel better about myself. I always tried to be the best at everything I did so that people would like me and accept me. But it was like Jesus came to me this last week and said, 'Jon, I made you, and I love you, and I don't care what you can *do*; I just want *you*. So now it's time for you to live for Me.' It was crazy! Because now, that's all I really want. I just want to serve Him!"

Madison couldn't help but smile at Jon's enthusiasm and passion. "That's great, Jon! Sounds like you're on the right track!"

Jon nodded eagerly. "Yeah. I mean, honestly, I'm still afraid this won't last, that I'll go back to where I was, but then I keep remembering that verse in Philippians, where it says, 'He who began a good work in you will be faithful to complete it...' Nothing depends on me. I just have to surrender to Him each day."

Madison and Charlotte couldn't help but look at each other with wonder and surprise on their faces.

Jon got louder. "I'm, like, totally excited to be back at camp! And I can't wait to tell my campers this week all about Jesus!"

A bright smile finally broke out on Charlotte's face. "Well, Jon, I think I believe you. I'll be praying that you have an amazing week with your cabin and that God continues to keep you on track and following Him."

"Thanks, Charlotte. And thanks, Maddy. I'll see you around!" He left the Program Office almost at a trot.

Charlotte and Madison looked at each other again in amazement. Madison said, "What just happened there?"

"Jesus. He's what happened there, I think!"

"*Amazing.*" Madison's eyes were wide open with surprise. "Well, miracles still happen! I hope it lasts..."

They laughed, looked at each other again, and then laughed some more.

"So," Madison began. "You were going to help me with my testimony?"

"Right. You're on tomorrow night at campfire?"

"Yeah. I'm *very* nervous! I've never had to do this before."

"Well, it's going to be great. I read over your testimony, and it's fantastic! I have just a couple of little things to suggest."

"Sure, I'd appreciate any help you can give."

"Well," Charlotte began, "what do you think the *purpose* of a testimony is?"

Madison thought for a moment. "Mmm. We went over this in staff training. To tell the kids your story? About how you met Jesus?"

"Well, yes and no. Obviously, you want to tell a *bit* of your story, but the overall purpose is to help the campers see how God has transformed your life. Really, it's not *your* story you want to tell, but *His* story you want to tell, and how His story has made a difference in your life."

"What do you mean? I thought my testimony was about me?"

Charlotte put down the pen she had been rolling between her fingers. "Yeah, it is about you, in a sense, but what I'm saying is that you have to choose what parts of your story you tell. We do that whenever we tell a story."

"Go on?"

Charlotte thought about how to explain it. "Look, if I tell you about my vacation to Fiji, I don't include all the parts about packing and sitting at the airport and putting on my makeup each morning, *unless* those help you understand what was really important to me on the trip. Instead, I tell you about the crazy people I met, the sunburn that almost put me in the hospital, and the cool waterfalls we visited. I have to pick and choose what's important."

"Okay, sure."

"So, in a testimony, what's most important for the campers to hear about?"

"Well, I guess they need to know who Jesus is and what He's done in my life."

"Exactly! So, choose the details that help bring *that* out to them."

"Yeah, that makes sense – I think. I guess I talked about a lot of stuff that wasn't too relevant, then, hey?"

Charlotte smiled, her dimples showing. "There may have been a few things that you could have left out. Like maybe the parts about your cat and that part about getting lost in the mall. Those are great stories, very interesting to tell in certain situations, but I don't think they necessarily add to the main point of how Jesus transformed your life."

Madison nodded, accepting the advice. "Well, okay, I can probably cut those out. How's the rest of it?"

"Great! I like your basic outline, where you broke it down to your life *before* Jesus, how you *met* Jesus – or how He transformed your life – and the *difference* He has made in your life ever since."

"Oh, good. Yeah, well, I just followed your basic outline from training, and it kinda made sense. I like the fact that the main point is supposed to be 'the difference Jesus made in my life.' Because then the campers can see that He can make a difference in their lives, too, right?"

"Exactly." She paused. "Actually, funny, now that I think about it, that's what Jon was doing, too, when he was here a few minutes ago. He talked about how he *used* to be so self-centered, how Jesus has been *changing* him, and how he's *now* so excited to tell kids about Jesus. He just gave us a two-minute testimony, if you look at it that way."

"Yeah, he did, didn't he?!" Madison exclaimed. "And it was all about what Jesus was doing in his life, not about *him* so much at all." She paused. "Is it that simple?"

"Yes, Maddy, it is. The whole point is to show that Jesus transforms lives and to give your life as an example. By the way, I really like the verse from Romans you used, too, about God being your Father."

"Thanks, Charlotte. Can I make some changes and then go over it with you tomorrow morning during my 'off' block?"

"Sure, Maddy! Let's do that."

"Thanks again. I'm off to archery in a few minutes, so I'd better go get myself ready. Have a great afternoon!"

Campfire had always been Madison's favorite part of the day as a camper. The crackle of the fire, the dancing flames, even the smell of the smoke that lingered on her clothes long afterward. She loved how the silly songs and skits gave way to the more meaningful songs, which in turn led to the speaker or a testimony given by one or two of the staff. Most of all she enjoyed just being together like one big family, singing and laughing and having fun. She found it magical.

But… it was even more than that: it was where Madison had felt the Spirit of God in a way like she had never before, and it was where she had given her life to Jesus, not too many years ago. Now, back as a cabin leader herself, she had the opportunity to help campers discover God's love for them.

Tonight, however, she felt like a nervous wreck. *Why did I say yes? Why didn't I just tell Charlotte that I can't speak in front of people, that I freeze up, that I would rather jump out of a plane than share at campfire? "I'll help you," she told me. Yeah, well, you're not going to be the one up here, are you? God, please help me!*

She tuned back in, and they were singing one of those "transitional" songs, a song that was still fun, but not ultra-hyper, to get the kids ready to sit and listen. *Why can't I go first and get it over with? But, no, Charlie gets to go first for some reason.*

Madison had only just met Charlie, as he had come as a volunteer for one week only, and she wasn't overly impressed with him. He seemed rather cocky. *Like most guys I know. Like Jon, but without the abilities! Oh, Lord, forgive me, and help me not to judge! Please help him to represent you well when he speaks tonight.*

The last chords of the song faded, and Meagan, who led campfires most nights, gave a short introduction to Charlie and then sat down on a bench. Charlie, a big smile on his face, jumped up, Bible in hand, and trotted up to the front.

He stood at the front, wiped his long bangs out of his eyes, looked at everyone, and after a drawn-out pause, said "Hey." A bunch of campers said "Hey" back to him.

"So, like, I'm just gonna give my testimony now, so listen up and pay attention. There's going to be a quiz at the end." Nobody laughed except Charlie, who gave a nervous chuckle.

"Most of you don't know me, but I was a camper here back in the day, and, like, it was awesome. I used to play tricks on my cabin all the time, like tying everyone's shoelaces together or greasing the toilet seat with Vaseline. It was great. If you need any ideas, just let me know, hey?" A few campers giggled a bit, but Madison wondered where he was going with his story.

"Anyway, I grew up with parents who didn't go to church, and my two older brothers picked on me all the time, so I was just glad that I got sent to camp every year, since it was the one place I didn't get picked on. In fact, I probably was the one picking on other kids at camp, since that was what I learned from my brothers and my dad, who used to hit me all the time." Some of the campers looked concerned. *Oh, man. Well, at least he has their attention?*

Charlie shuffled nervously and moved his hair from his eyes again. "I remember one time when I had forgotten to bring home my homework from school, he took a stick and hit me so hard, I had these huge welts on my butt. It was so terrifying, and I couldn't sit down for days without incredible pain. And one time, he pushed me into a wall, and I jammed my finger and busted it. He made me tell the nurse at the hospital that I had done it playing basketball." All the kids were totally silent, and a couple that Madison could see looked very anxious.

Charlie suddenly spoke very loudly and intensely. "'Smarten up, Charlie! Don't be such a baby, Charlie! Why can't you be like your brothers, Charlie! You're no good for anything, Charlie!' That's all I ever heard from my dad!" In the firelight, Charlie's eyes were intense but sad, and Madison hoped he would settle down and stop frightening the kids so much.

But Charlie wasn't done, and for the next two or three minutes, he continued to talk about his relationship with his dad and how bad it had been. By now, a couple of kids were sobbing quietly, and the mood was becoming more and more awkward by the moment.

Then he started talking about the substance abuse he struggled with throughout his teen years, and Madison could see Meagan was trying subtly to get his attention without the campers noticing, but it wasn't working. Finally, she had to interrupt him. "Hey, Charlie, you're going to need to wrap this up soon, hey?"

He looked briefly perturbed, but he recovered quickly, if somewhat sarcastically. "Oh, yeah, good idea. Don't want to take more than my *allotted* time." He paused, trying to collect himself and his thoughts.

"So, anyway, you guys, that's why camp made such a difference in my life. My dad wasn't here, I wasn't tempted by drugs here – except that one time I tried to smuggle some in and got caught! – and I could be myself. But, honestly, I hated myself, and even at camp, I was doing things to harm myself and others. But then they kept talking about Jesus and how He would make everything better, so in my, let me see, in my, uh, third year, no, my fourth year coming here, I said the prayer, asked Jesus into my heart, and all that. So, now I'm a Christian, and life is still pretty hard, but at least I know I'm going to heaven. So, yeah, you guys, keep listening to the speaker and maybe ask somebody if you have questions because being a Christian is *awesome*! *Yeah*!"

Charlie pumped his fist and went to sit down, and some of the campers clapped enthusiastically, though Madison wasn't sure if it was for him or more because they were so glad that he was done. *Well, how do I follow that, Lord? Help me to honor you with my talk.*

Meagan was now up front with her guitar again. "Thanks, Charlie, for sharing with us. The Christian life isn't easy, but when we put our trust in Jesus, He makes us brand new. We're going to sing one more song, and then we're going to invite *Maddy* up to share with us!" A few kids cheered, mostly from Madison's cabin, and Meagan began the song.

Afterwards, Madison couldn't even remember what song had been sung, but soon she found herself introduced and up front. She hoped no one could see her knees or hands shaking. *Get it together, girl, you can do this!* But could she? And then she remembered what Charlotte had told her. "The best way to get over nervousness is to be passionate about your subject. And I know you love Jesus and His good news, so think about how amazing it will be to share with these kids the difference that Jesus has made in your life." *Yeah, that's why I'm here. It's all about You, Jesus!*

"Have you guys ever wondered why you're on this planet? I don't mean why you weren't born on, like, Neptune or Mars, since that would be kinda awkward, but have you ever wondered if there was a *purpose* for your life? That's how I felt growing up. I always wondered why I was here." Even through the haze of the campfire smoke, Madison could see a few kids nodding, and she felt like they were with her already. *We can do this, Jesus!*

"I was born at a pretty young age, as we all were…" A couple of kids laughed as she continued. "…but I'm telling you, it was tough growing up as an only child to a single mom. We didn't have much money or a lot of the stuff other people had; we only had each other, and that wasn't even great because my mom always had to work, which meant she often had to leave me with her friends." *This is going to be okay.*

"I had trouble making friends at school, probably partly because we moved a lot, and I can remember so many times when I was lonely and just didn't have anyone to go to. I began to feel like there was something wrong with me. But when I came to camp for the first time, when I was nine years old, I felt like there was something different here."

The fire sparked suddenly, and a few campers jumped a little, but they settled down quickly, to Madison's relief. "The activities were lots of fun, of course, but it was more than that. I just remember my cabin leader, her name was Rebecca, and she was always so full of joy, even when we kept her awake half the night, and when she talked about Jesus, it was like she really *knew* Him and *loved* Him."

Madison took a quick peek down at the notes she had in her Bible and then continued. "Even at nine years old, I was struggling with this whole idea of purpose and meaning in life, and I remember one night Rebecca shared about some of her struggles and how she had found everything she needed in life through her relationship with Jesus. And she talked about how Jesus was God and how He loved us so much that He came down to earth as a man, lived a perfect life, and died on a cross to pay the penalty for all our sins. And how we could have a relationship with God by putting our trust in Him."

Madison looked into the eyes of a few of the kids near the front and could see they were listening intently. "Deep inside me, I knew that was what I wanted and needed, but to be honest, at nine years old there were a bunch of things that didn't make sense, yet. I remember talking to my cabin leader and asking a zillion questions, and she told me that whenever I was ready, Jesus was waiting for me, arms open wide." *Was He ever!*

"But I wasn't quite there that year. It made sense, but I guess I just had to be sure. And then my life took a huge turn for the worse. Not long after I got home from camp, my mom started to get really sick, and it turned out she had cancer, and for the next two years, it was like I was walking through this fog of fears and crying and emotions I didn't know how to deal with. But even in that terrible time, somehow I knew that God was still out there and still cared and still wanted me to become His child."

She had momentum now. "You see, I'd never had a dad, and I guess it was my second year of camp when I learned that God would be my dad if I trusted in Him. That meant so much to me. Well, to make a long story not quite so long, my mom came through all the treatments, and in my third year of camp, guess what, I had Rebecca as my cabin leader again! I totally remember being at campfire on the last night, and I was full of tears and emotions, finally ready to give my life to Jesus. And so I prayed with Rebecca, told God how sorry I was for all the things I had done wrong, thanked Him for sending Jesus to die for me, and told Him that I wanted to be His child and to follow Him for the rest of my life!"

The smoke from the campfire enveloped her, and she moved a little to her left to escape it. "It was an emotional time, and maybe I expected things to change right away, but to be honest, they didn't. I went home after camp, and I still had very few friends. I did persuade my mom to start taking me to church, and there were some kids' programs I went to that helped me learn more about Jesus and the Bible. And I made a few friends there, too."

"Life has still been a struggle in the years since then. My mom is back in treatments for cancer again, and without Jesus, I don't know if I would've made it. I certainly wouldn't be here talking to you! I have to tell you that I have this amazing peace God gives me in the midst of all this stuff I'm dealing with. He walks with me day by day, no matter what I face." Even in the smoky haze, Madison's face was radiant.

"I want to share with you one verse that has come to mean a lot to me." Madison looked down at her Bible. "It's found in Romans 8:15, and it says this:

> So you have not received a spirit that makes you fearful slaves. Instead, you received God's Spirit when he adopted you as his own children. Now we call him, "Abba, Father."

"'Abba' means 'daddy,' so this verse says I can have a very personal relationship with the God of the universe! I can't tell you all that means to me, to be adopted as a child of God, and to not need to fear. I used to be afraid of everything, especially for my mom, but now I know God is in control, even when I don't understand what's going on."

Madison flipped some pages. "Let me leave you with one more verse. John 1:10-12 says,

> He came into the very world he created, but the world didn't recognize him. He came to his own people, and even they rejected him. But to all who believed him and accepted him, he gave the right to become children of God.

She exclaimed, more loudly than she meant to, "Isn't that *amazing*! If we believe in Jesus and receive Him as our Lord and Savior, He says we become His children!" Maddy paused while she closed her Bible.

"So, I just want to encourage you. If you feel lonely or not sure why you're even on this planet, know that God loves you and wants you to become His child. He will give your life meaning and purpose. *Forever*! Thanks for listening."

Madison sat down, and the kids applauded loudly. *Wow, thank you, Lord! We made it through!*

Meagan stood up with her guitar. "I've got nothing to add to that. Thanks, Maddy, awesome job. And we'll pray for your mom. In fact, let's do that right now…"

Debriefing

GIVING A TESTIMONY is one of the most powerful ways to portray the gospel to campers – or to anyone you meet. It's personal, it's relatable, and it's not easy for people to argue with or discount. They can tell you your view of the Bible is wrong or that your pastor is wrong, but when you talk about your own experiences, that often connects strongly with people.

For many years, I have been teaching people how to give testimonies at camp, and I find a lot of people have some kind of mental block when it comes time to write it out. There are at least two reasons for this: first, because people think it's going to be harder than it is, and second, because if you haven't truly had an encounter with Jesus, it's rather difficult to write about it.

The second problem I can't fix, other than to encourage them to keep seeking God, Who promises that those who truly seek Him will find Him. However, for the first problem, I believe that it's just a matter of breaking it down into a few simple concepts.

Just One Thing

When writing any kind of talk (or really anything at all), first decide what the *main* thing is. What is the one (not three, but *one*) concept, idea, or truth you are trying to convey? Everything else should contribute to that one main thing.

An evangelistic testimony makes it very simple to know what that one thing is: "The difference Jesus made in my life." Your testimony isn't about *you* at all – it's about *Jesus* and His transformational work in your life.

A Life-Saving Appendectomy

If you want to know the difference something or someone made, the easiest way to define that is by showing what something was like before and after. For example, let me tell you how I ended up with no appendix. It's quite simple. I was born with an appendix, and I lived quite happily with it for many years, though it seemed to do little for me that I knew about. One day, however, I started experiencing pain in that region, so a surgeon cut me open and removed it. It was a painful healing process, but it saved my life. Now I have no appendix, and I won't die from appendicitis. I was saved!

Before my surgery, I was in much pain and in danger of dying. *Afterwards*, I was safe and without pain. What made the difference? A doctor cut me open and took away my appendix! Praise God!

Granted, that's a weird example, but similarly, my testimony is about the difference Jesus made in my life. At one time, I had a terrible temper and got in lots of fights. I lived for myself. The most important thing in my life was soccer and other athletic pursuits. Though I didn't know it, I was separated from God by all my sin. Today, however, I am living for God, and the most important things in my life have everything to do with serving Him and helping others to know Him and grow in their relationship with Him.

The difference? Jesus came along, loved me, and showed me that I could be forgiven, set free, and live a life worth living. I learned that He died on the cross to pay for my sins, that He rose again to conquer death, and that, according to the Bible, if I put my trust in Him alone, I would be given eternal life and made into a new person. So, that's what I did, and now I'm a brand-new man. I'm saved!

A simple structure for a testimony is as follows:

1. What was my life like before I met Jesus?
2. What changed? How did that happen?
3. What has my life been like since Jesus rescued me?

This structure keeps *Jesus* at the center of our testimony, and the details we add from our own life and experience all contribute to the main point: the difference Jesus has made in my life.

I have put a testimony worksheet in Appendix B to help you with this. Not to be confused with my missing appendix, this one should be there.

The Early Conversion Quandary

Some people will say, "But I didn't really *have* a life before I met Jesus because I was four years old when I first received His salvation!"

That is true of many people. However, the question, then, is this: did you, from the time you were four, always live for Him? If not, what happened to make *that* change?

You see, that's my story, too. I grew up in a Christian home and trusted in Jesus at a very young age. But for the next number of years, though I was probably "saved," I wasn't living for Jesus. Some significant things changed in my life. I won't go into them here, but they involved youth leaders God put in my life and experiences at camp that broke me and caused me to change direction and take my faith seriously (and ultimately head to Bible school and into ministry).

So, my emphasis on my early years isn't the years leading up to when I was four (I remember little of those years, surprisingly enough), but rather the years that led up to deciding to start following Jesus truly.

Final Tips

Here are a few more simple things to consider when you are writing a testimony:

1. **Planning & Preparing**

   - Always be aware of your audience, considering their age and spiritual development.

   - Re-write your testimony a little every time you give it so that it will be fresh to you.

   - Aim for about 3-5 minutes total. This will force you to be concise.

   - Plan the whole testimony around one simple idea: how Jesus has transformed your life. This will normally lend itself to a structure that shows how things were, what changed, and how things are today.

   - Avoid using "Christian-ese," i.e., language or clichés that campers will not understand (e.g., "I was redeemed by the blood of the Lamb, sanctified by His grace!"). Even words like "sin" may need to be defined (e.g., "doing what you know to be wrong" for younger kids).

- Avoid putting down churches, organizations, or people who may have hurt you along the way.

- Avoid glorifying sin. Better to talk about the consequences you and others around you suffered from your sin than the enjoyment you had while in it.

- It is often very helpful to share a verse or two from the Bible that connect with what you are talking about and may have been meaningful to you recently or on your journey.

- Be clear in your testimony on how you were saved: through faith, by God's grace, based on the sacrifice of Jesus on the cross.

- Be genuine. Don't pretend the Christian life is easy or perfect.

- Practice in front of a friend if possible and ask for genuine feedback. It is also helpful to practice in front of a mirror.

- Pray into your testimony from the time of preparing through the time of delivery, and even afterward, knowing that it will only be effective to the degree that God works through it.

- Remember: If you do not talk about Jesus Christ in your testimony, it is not a Christian testimony!

2. **Presenting**

- Ask friends to pray for you while you present, and ask God to speak through your words.

- Get people's attention with your introduction. Sometimes it can be effective to use a question like, "Have you ever felt like nobody cared about you?" or "Do you ever look out at the stars and wonder how they got there?"

- Saying something humorous at the beginning will usually help both you and your audience relax.

- Be passionate about what you are saying; that also will help you overcome your nervousness.

- Be positive and enthusiastic about your story, especially about what Jesus has done for you.

- Avoid nervous habits like clicking a pen, clearing your throat, saying "um," and so on. In fact, avoid having anything in your hands that you might unknowingly play with.

- Speak clearly and slowly – don't rush!

- Don't feel like you need to convince people to believe. Your role is simply to be a witness to what God has done in your life. It is up to the Holy Spirit to convict people.

- Come to a definite conclusion, rather than just fading off and saying something like, "Well, I guess that's it." Better to finish positively with something like, "So that's the difference Jesus has made in my life, and I hope that you will get to know Him, too."

- Thank God for the opportunity to give your testimony, and pray that He would use it to draw people closer to Him.

- Ask for realistic feedback from someone you trust, so that you can continue to improve.

Testimonies don't have to be intimidating. All you're doing is giving witness to what Jesus has done in your life, and that should be a joy and a privilege, not a chore. Use these simple tips, "And if someone asks about your hope as a believer, always be ready to explain it." (1 Peter 3:15b). Go get 'em!

Discussion Questions

1. What was missing from Charlie's testimony? What parts were unnecessary or unhelpful?

2. Why do you think giving a testimony can be such a powerful way of witnessing to campers about who Jesus is?

3. What should the main point of a Christian testimony be? Why?

4. How can you talk about your "life before meeting Jesus" if you believed at a young age?

5. Why do you think it is important not to "glorify sin" when giving your testimony?

6. What are some good ways to prepare yourself for giving your testimony?

7. Why would you say that prayer is so important in the preparation and presentation of a testimony?

8. What do you see as the hardest part of writing your testimony? Why?

NEXT STEPS

CHAPTER 14

Servant Hearts & New Beginnings
Life After Camp

MADDY!"
Madison was jolted from her day-dreaming and looked up.
What? I heard my name. What did I do? People were clapping and cheering and looking at her. *What?*

"Come on up, Madison, and receive your award!"
Charlotte? What's going on? Oh, wow, did I receive an award for something? She rose, bewildered, from her chair and headed to the front.

It had been a long summer, and Madison was exhausted. Camp had ended yesterday, and she couldn't believe how sad she was to see her last cabin of girls head home. At the beginning of the week, she thought she would be glad to see the backs of those fifteen and sixteen-year-old teens – they were so mean to each other, and to her! But by the end, they not only were getting along great as a cabin, but two of them had also given their lives to Jesus!

It had been *such* an emotional roller-coaster, and she felt like she would need to sleep for weeks before feeling refreshed. She had slept ten hours last night all by herself in her cabin, yet her whole body still ached with exhaustion, her head felt fuzzy inside, and she had been fighting to keep her eyes open during the final ceremonies and awards service.

Charlotte was talking about her as she struggled to make her way through the chairs and people to the front. "What a privilege it has been for me to get to know Maddy this summer. She knew hardly anyone at all when she arrived ten weeks ago, but I think we've all seen her touching the lives of everyone in this room, one way or another." Charlotte paused, and Madison could see people nodding in the audience.

Really? I did so little. That was You, Jesus!

"Funny, though, as I have gotten to know Madison, I have realized that the last thing she would want would be to stand up here in front of you, receiving recognition, because she prefers to serve in the background where no one will notice her."

That's for sure. Can I please sit down now?!

"But I think it's important, for the sake of the team, that we point out when people are doing the kinds of things that we have been encouraging you to do all summer. So often, we point out the mistakes we make, or we try to correct people's behaviors, but we also need to remember and rejoice when people do a great job in a particular area and celebrate the way God is working among us. The New Testament writers, especially Paul, often pointed to the examples of certain people and said, 'Look, live like this.' In fact, Paul even pointed to himself and told his readers to follow his example, just as he followed the example of Jesus."

Madison made it to the front and sheepishly looked around. Several of the staff smiled, and one guy gave her the "thumbs up." She could see Bruce standing at the back with a big smile on his face. Her heart was pounding, a lot like it was when she gave her testimony.

Charlotte continued. "The truth is, many of you could have received this award. There have been so many acts of servanthood throughout this summer, so many times when each of you has set a good example by following Jesus and putting others and their needs ahead of yourselves. That's what it means to serve God at camp, and we're so thankful for the sacrifices you have made this summer.

"Maddy, however, has done this so incredibly consistently, all summer. She came to camp all nervous and scared and feeling like she just couldn't do it. But she constantly chose to put her trust in God, instead of herself, and she chose to give everything she had to these campers and to all of us. She became a top-notch cabin leader, in spite of her inexperience and fears, and I think it was simply because she continually gave it all to God. She surrendered to His Spirit living in her, day after day."

Or, I just had no idea what I was doing and stumbled my way through the summer!

"So, Maddy, on behalf of the leadership team, I present to you this plaque, the 'Servant's Heart' award! Well done!" Everyone clapped, and many cheered out loud. Madison felt the blood rush to her face, and she looked down at the ground while muttering her thanks. She walked back to her chair in a daze.

There were a few more awards given out, another song, and then Bruce ended off with a long (but sincere) prayer for all of them. And then summer was officially over!

Madison could see Jon making his way over to her.

Oh dear, what now? Oh, wait, he's better now. I hope.

"Maddy! Congrats on the award!" Jon's big, warm smile disarmed her immediately.

"Thanks, Jon. I - I didn't deserve it, but it's nice to be thought of."

"Well, I disagree, but I know it's hard to accept praise sometimes."

"Yeah, well, yeah. I just want to make sure the praise goes to God, not to me, because, really, I don't feel like I did much this summer except limp from one crisis to another. It was a *long* race, and I feel like I stumbled over the finish line this week."

Jon nodded, a big smile still on his face. "So, now what? You're heading back to school?"

"Yup. First-year nursing."

"Cool. I'll be back at Bible college for my third year. Man, I am so excited to go back!"

"How come? I mean, that's good, but don't you find school to be a lot of work, especially in college?"

"Yeah, I guess so." Jon cocked his head slightly, thinking. After a short pause, he said, "I think I went to college my first year just wanting to have fun, and I, uh, got suspended for some of that fun, actually. And then last year, I didn't get in so much trouble, but I didn't take my studies seriously at all, and I wasted a lot of time and money. The truth is, I wasn't even going to go back this year, but, man, am I ever glad I changed my mind in time!"

Madison was curious. "Well, what changed? You've been so . . . *different* lately. Was that just from having that week or so off?"

"*Everything* changed! *Me*! My perspective, my relationship with God. These last two weeks of summer have been *amazing* in my cabins! Probably harder than usual, but *so* good!" He suddenly sobered. "Let me tell you a little secret. This is my third year counseling and my fifth year helping out at camp. But until two weeks ago, I had *never* led a camper to Christ. Not once."

Madison couldn't hold back her surprise. "Really?! Not that we can ever know when God will give us those opportunities, but that must've been tough."

"But that's the thing – I honestly didn't care. Being at camp was all about *me*, and being a cabin leader was just the thing I had to do to be here. Kids annoyed me, especially the bratty ones, but I learned how to control them for the most part, so it looked like everything was good in my cabins."

"You were faking it? You don't even like kids?"

Jon quickly reacted to what felt like an accusation. "Well, no, I'm not saying *that*. Give me a little credit, will you?"

Madison looked stung by Jon's response but said nothing.

"Oh, sorry, Maddy, I . . . I'm just a little defensive. I'm trying to change, but it's hard. I hate the way I acted, and I want to be better."

Madison recovered quickly and said, "That's okay, Jon. I'm just trying to understand how you managed to serve at camp when your heart wasn't in it."

"Yeah, that's the thing. I guess, well, yeah, maybe some of the time I *was* faking it. I do like most kids, and part of me really wanted to see them grow and put their faith in Jesus, but it just wasn't my number one priority. Like I said, I've been pretty self-centered, but God has truly been teaching me these last few weeks, and it was so different being a cabin leader when I cared. And at least three kids came to Christ in the last two weeks in my cabins!"

"That's so great, Jon! I'm so glad for you. And for them! I'm glad you're excited to go back to school. I'm just nervous that I'll be able to handle college."

Jon flashed a smile. "Oh, you'll do great! Just make sure you're taking courses you care about. I'm excited to get back into studying the Bible and theology. Now that I feel like I'm getting to know Jesus more, I think it's all going to be that much more meaningful."

"Yeah, well, I really want to be a nurse, so I'm sure the courses will be good." Madison paused. "But Jon, let me ask you this: aren't you afraid that the hype of summer is going to fade? That you'll go back to where you were before the summer? You said something about that in Charlotte's office."

Jon looked up and then straight into Madison's eyes. "For sure, that's a fear of mine. But I've been able to connect already with a godly older man at the college who has agreed to mentor me and keep me accountable, and I think that's going to help."

Madison sighed. "I wish I had someone like that."

"What about Charlotte? She's at your school, too, isn't she?"

"Yeah, but she's too busy…"

"Well, maybe, but she likes you, and I bet she would mentor you if you asked."

Madison paused as she thought about that. "Well, I guess I can always ask. Yeah, maybe I will. I just don't want to lose all of this." She gestured at the camp in general. "I just don't want things to go bad when I get back to the real world."

"Well," Jon began, "don't you think what we experienced this summer was real?"

"Yeah, but…"

"So, maybe *this* is the real world, and we're going back to the fake world."

"Uh, okay, maybe? What do you mean?"

Jon's voice raised passionately. "Maddy, I used to think this was a little bubble, here at camp, and then I'd go back to 'reality' after the summer and find things in the 'real' world were so different. But then it occurred to me, just last week, actually, that the spiritual battles we fought here, the community we experienced, the way we saw God work in our lives and in the lives of the campers, well, that's *reality*. That's more like how God intended us to live. And then we go home to the plastic, fake world of shopping malls, television, fashions, media, and all that crap we get inundated with. So, which is more 'real'?" He shrugged. "Somehow, I want to take camp home with me."

Madison felt like a light turned on in her head. "You're right, Jon! I think this *is* the real world here in a lot of ways!" She thought for a moment. "But maybe it's not *camp* we need to take home with us, but

God's Spirit. He dwells with us wherever we go, but somehow at camp we feel His presence so much more."

Jon nodded. "Yeah, and I think that's because there are way fewer distractions here at camp. And because we're forced to depend on Him more." He closed his eyes suddenly and began to pray. "Lord, may we depend on You wherever we go and live undistracted lives at home and at college, where our focus is always and only on You!"

Madison had to smile at Jon's enthusiastic prayer. "Amen to that! Well, Jon, it's been nice getting to know you a little bit this summer, especially these last couple of weeks. Have a great year! Think you'll be back next summer?"

"I sure hope so. You?"

"God willing, I wouldn't miss it!"

An awkward moment ensued where Madison was afraid Jon would try to give her a hug, but he backed off, smiled and gave a small wave as he headed out the door of the chapel. A few others were still milling around, focused on each other, telling stories and saying their goodbyes.

Well, Lord, I guess you knew what you were doing. Thanks for an amazing summer. You sure taught me a lot! I'm going to miss this place and these people, but I'm so glad that You're going with me. Help me to keep it real!

Debriefing

I ALWAYS FOUND the last day of camp to be extremely emotional and difficult. It was hard to leave friends who I loved and with whom I had worked side by side, all summer long, through all the tough times. And I did feel as though getting back to the "real world" was pretty tough after all I had experienced during the summer.

But when I think of this world, where the curse of the Fall is so evident everywhere we look, and then I think of Eden, the perfect world before the Fall, and I read about the New Heaven and the New Earth, it makes me wonder: isn't camp more like the world we came from and the world that God is preparing for us? Maybe camp is more "real" than our "normal" lives away from camp.

Granted, camp work is hard, and we mess up, and things go wrong, and sometimes we are hurt by what people say or do. That's still part of the fake, cursed world we're going to leave behind. But camp is also the place where I have been able to be myself and use my gifts and commune with God and others in ways that I have never been able to do anywhere else. So maybe it would be best to describe camp as a small window we can peer through into the reality yet to come. And that thought makes me so excited about the coming world – a bit like camp, but so much better!

So, an important question to consider is this: when you leave camp, what can you do to keep following Jesus like you learned to do at camp? How can you continue to be "real" in a fake world? Here are a few ideas that may help you:

1. Find a mentor

Probably the one thing we all need the most yet have the hardest time doing is finding a mentor, someone who will build into your life and keep you accountable.

Ideally, you want to find someone who is significantly older in the faith than you are, someone you can totally trust, and someone who has more life experience than you have. Ask them to meet with you regularly, whether it is once per week, once every month, or even every couple of months. Ask them to pray for you. And most importantly, ask them to ask *you* tough questions about what you've been doing, where you've been going, how you've been spending your time and money, and so on. They should be given permission to correct you as needed, and hopefully to constantly encourage you as well.

Having a mentor who is truly willing to invest in you is something that increases your chances of success in life by many times. I know in my own life, just the knowledge that I am being kept accountable, that someone will be asking me the tough questions about my personal life, my purity, my attitudes, my devotional practices, and so on – this has greatly helped to keep me on track.

If you see someone you want to be like, get close to them. If necessary, push your way into their life! Spend time with them; get their permission to learn from them. Ask them to mentor you. They may say "no," but keep trying until you find someone who is willing. Don't look for someone who is perfect, but find someone who is enthusiastically pursuing Jesus.

2. Become active in a local church

Another form of accountability that we all need in our lives is the local church, especially if you can serve there and get involved in a small group that meets regularly. Don't think of the church as a man-made institution; it was *God's* idea. He has promised to build it, both in the sense of the universal body of believers and in the sense of small pockets of believers who meet regularly for worship, teaching from His Word, the exercising of spiritual gifts (within and without the church), baptism, and the Lord's supper.

Not only do you need the church, but the church needs you as well. If you are holding back your gifts, it is like a body that is injured or missing a part. As Hebrews 10:24-25 reminds us,

> Let us think of ways to motivate one another to acts of love and good works. And let us not neglect our meeting together, as some people do, but encourage one another, especially now that the day of his return is drawing near.

The end of this age is approaching, and Jesus is coming back! In the meantime, God calls us to meet as His Church and do His work in this world – together. Never expect to find a perfect church. Since churches are made up of people like you and me, churches will never be perfect until Jesus returns and we are finally changed into His image. We don't need a perfect church, but we do need one whose leadership is faithful to the Word of God and to the leading of the Holy Spirit.

3. Gain competencies and learn skills

Always be a student, even after your school days are over. The more skills you have, the more useful you can be in God's service.

Simple things like picking up cooking skills and a Food Safe course (in my part of the world) will come in very handy when someone is suddenly needed to help feed the homeless in your area. If you're a decent swimmer, consider getting certified as a lifeguard. Take the highest level of first-aid you can afford, and re-certify regularly. Learn to sew, change tires on a car, do basic auto mechanics, woodworking, welding, photography, graphic design, public speaking, plumbing, accounting, construction, and so on. Help coach a sports team.

Every one of these skills can be used in ministry. Even at camp, we constantly need people who can do these sorts of things. Years ago, I got my license to drive a bus, and many times it has come in very handy. My soccer refereeing and my coaching experiences have helped me deal confidently with people and think through how to run games, making sure they are safe and fair for campers.

Be a learner. Think less in terms of degrees (unless they are required for a certain position you want to pursue) than in terms of skills and competencies. Employers are generally less impressed with what you know than what you can do, but more importantly, the more you can do, the more help you're going to be to those around you.

4. Become adaptable

Similarly, learn to adapt to your surroundings. Things change so quickly these days that those who can adapt often succeed where other very skilled, non-adapting people fail.

And this is again why a wide variety of skills is helpful wherever you go. Chances are that you won't be doing the same work or ministry for 20-40 years like most of our ancestors did. Always keep your eyes open for opportunities to change and grow.

5. Develop character

While we tend to blame most of our failings on outside problems or someone else's mistakes, they often come back to who we are – our character. Apparently, the number one reason foreign missionaries quit and come home is that they are unable to get along with the other missionaries. How sad to be called to a ministry, whether at home or far away, only to give up because of relational problems with others in the ministry!

Character is developed slowly over the course of much time and many decisions. Often, we see people making what seems like a single horrendous choice that hurts them and those around them. However, that one choice is almost always the result of many previous poor choices along the way.

Carefully choose your friends and what you expose your mind and eyes to. Be aware of all the little decisions and compromises you make. If you spend lots of time in God's word, with godly people, in positive places, and where godliness is practiced and taught, you will almost certainly become godly over time. The opposite is also true. As the little song I was taught in Sunday school says, "Oh, be careful little feet where you go..."

Because character is developed in the moment by moment choices you make, the best time to correct your path is when you first mess up. It's like dieting – if you suddenly binge and eat a full box of cookies, it's easy to say, well, I've blown it now, so I might as well have some cake and ice cream, too. But the best thing you can do when you've done something you regret is to determine to start fresh from *right now* and do the right thing from this point forward.

6. Take risks

I have read and heard that the number one thing older people regret is that they missed opportunities because they took too few risks when they were younger. They're not talking about jumping out of airplanes (though they may regret being too afraid to do that, too), but more in terms of being too afraid to fail or not investing enough in relationships, fearing hurt or rejection.

Everyone is going to make mistakes, and those who "go for it" in life don't necessarily make more mistakes, they just get more out of life. We tend to ask ourselves – what is the *worst* that could happen? And then we shy away from it. But instead, try asking yourself – what is the *best* thing that could happen here? Is that worth giving it a try?

Also, be realistic as to how hard it would be to recover if things go wrong and it doesn't work out. Is this a risk worth taking? Don't ever take risks "just for the thrill of it," and be sure that the purpose of taking a risk falls in with God's purpose for your life.

7. Learn from failure

I hate to fail, but I love the lessons I have learned from failure! I truly do. And without taking risks, I never would have failed, and I would have continued to be afraid of failing. But those who choose to learn from failure, those who jump back up and try again or in a different way, those people are the ones who accomplish so much more than the rest who were afraid to fail.

I've called it "failing forward" in this book. I don't know who first coined that expression, but it's become a favorite of mine. So many people look at failure as falling backward, as regressing, as hurting their progress, but when successful people fail, they spend time considering carefully what went wrong, how they can improve, what resources they lacked last time, and so on. Then they try again. And again.

8. Confront the truth about yourself

Consider carefully who you are, what your limitations are, and what you are truly good at. Ask your friends, family, and co-workers questions like: What do you think I'm good at? What do you think I could improve on? If you were to pick a career for me, what would it be? Do personality style tests, and have others do them for you. Admit to yourself the areas you need to improve in, the areas you really aren't going to improve in, and the areas where you are capable or strong.

I am not saying you should spend lots of time "gazing at your navel," thinking about yourself, but there are times to take a good, long, hard look to discover if you are heading in the right direction. There are too many people who spend many years and a fortune in college or university, taking courses that they will never use for anything more than getting a slip of paper saying they completed all those courses. Or hoping for a music career when they lack talent. Or studying to be a pastor only to find out that they would never be a good pastor. Or becoming an elementary school teacher when they don't like kids. Those people are often stuck for years where they shouldn't be.

If only they had confronted the "brutal facts" or asked someone to help them do that! What are you genuinely good at and passionate about? Instead of simply wasting time and money on an "education," maybe start by talking to people who know you well. And then try things. Teach a class at your church and see if you love teaching. Perform in front of a talented musician and ask for their true opinion. Serve in various places to see if these are things that bring you joy and bring God glory. Then, when you know what God has wired you to do, choose an education that will help you improve in those areas.

Camp is, of course, a great place to do many of these things, which is yet another reason I love camp so much!

Finally

Some have suggested to me that Jon's turn-around seems a little unrealistic, and you might agree. I know in my own life there have been very few sudden changes in the attitudes and habits that I have prayed would change. Those changes usually take a long time.

But it *does* happen. The Apostle Paul is an example from Scripture, and many others have been changed instantly by God's mighty Spirit working in them. Many addicts have met Jesus and lost all cravings for their drugs, and there are many people, even today, who have been instantly physically healed in Jesus' name. I've read numerous stories about those who hated God but made a 180-degree turn to follow Jesus and serve Him as missionaries.

Miracles still happen, and God will change each of us, in His perfect timing, if we pursue Him with all our hearts. In the meantime, let's not let our imperfections keep us from doing the good works God has planned for us to do in His name (Ephesians 2:10).

Most of all, let us never forget or lose sight of the fact that Jesus is coming back! We have no idea how much time we have until our opportunities for reaching the lost are gone forever. The fields are "white unto harvest," and Jesus desires workers to get out there and tell people about Him!

Camp is one such place where this happens naturally and often, but there are many other places to serve. My hope for you is that you will truly seek after God and serve Him wherever you go. The opportunities are all around us. We just have to pray that God will give us the eyes to see people and situations as He sees them, and then we need to obey Him and share God's love wherever we go.

God has truly blessed me and millions of other campers and staff members through camp ministry. I pray that it will be a blessing to you, as well, and that you will be a blessing wherever you go from here. Seize the day!

Discussion Questions

1. Do you think that Jon's turn-around was realistic? Why or why not? Do we limit God when we doubt His ability to change us or others?

2. Do you think camp or non-camp is more like the "real" world? In what ways could each be defined that way?

3. Why do you think it is often so hard to leave camp at the end of a summer of serving there?

4. What are some steps you (personally) need to take to continue to grow in your faith apart from camp?

5. What are some skills you would like to pick up over the next few years? How will you do that?

6. When you think about your character and how it has developed over the past few months, are you satisfied? Why or why not? Are there decisions you will need to make differently in the future?

7. Are you considering finding a mentor? Do you have ideas of who you might approach? Is there anyone *you* should be mentoring?

8. Are there brutal facts in your life that you need to confront? How can proper accountability help you to do this?

9. Having read this book, what *should* you do in the next 24 hours to move forward with the knowledge you have gained? What *will* you do, and who will keep you accountable to do that?

APPENDICES

APPENDIX A

A Simple Gospel Presentation

GOD'S PURPOSE: LIFE

God created us to live a full life in relationship to Him.

- Genesis 1:27   God created us in His image
- Psalm 139:13-16   God formed us and knows us completely
- Isaiah 43:7   God created us to bring Him glory
- Ephesians 1:4-5   God created us for a relationship with Him
- John 10:10b   Jesus came to provide a full, abundant life
- Ephesians 2:10   We are created as God's masterpieces to do good works

OUR PROBLEM: SIN

Rebellion has separated us from God

- Genesis 2:17, 3:17 Evil entered the world by our disobedience
- Isaiah 59:2   Our rebellion separates us from God
- Romans 3:10, 23   Every person has sinned and experiences separation

Rebellion results in death and judgment

- Romans 1:18-19   Sinful people are already under God's wrath
- Romans 6:23a   Sin always results in death
- Hebrews 9:27   All people will one day face judgment
- Proverbs 14:12   Our attempts to do right still result in death

GOD'S REMEDY: JESUS

God gave His Son Jesus to pay the penalty for our rebellion

- 1 Peter 2:24   Jesus bore our sins on the cross to heal us of our sins
- Romans 6:23b   Jesus provides a free gift of eternal life
- Romans 5:8   Jesus died in our place out of love for us
- Hebrews 10:12   Jesus offered, for all time, a single, perfect, sacrifice for sins
- John 14:6   Jesus is the only way to God
- 1 Peter 1:3   Jesus' resurrection from the dead has brought new life and new hope

OUR RESPONSE: BELIEVE & RECEIVE

Each person must individually receive the gift of life through faith

- Mark 1:15   True faith includes repentance (turning away from sin)
- Romans 10:9-10   True faith submits to Jesus as our Lord (master)
- John 1:12   Those who believe become God's children
- John 3:16, 17, 36   Whoever believes in Jesus has eternal life
- John 5:24   Belief in Jesus bridges the gap between us and God
- John 11:25   Through Jesus' death and resurrection, all who believe in Jesus will live forever
- 1 John 5: 11-13   Those who have Jesus have eternal life (now!)
- Ephesians 2:8-9   Saved by God's grace through faith, not by any kind of work
- Romans 8:1   Confidence that if we trust Jesus, we are no longer condemned

APPENDIX B

Testimony Worksheet

Introduction
- How can you get their attention and get yourself comfortable?

Part I – Life before Christ
- What was life like before you trusted Christ?

- If you trusted Jesus at a young age, what was your life like before you truly began to live for Him?

- What kinds of attitudes did you have?

- What was important to you, what were your goals in life?

- What was not satisfying about that life?

Part II – Heart Change
- What began to change in your life to lead you to trust Christ?

- What was the turning point in your life?

- When did you hear the gospel, and how did it affect you, how did you respond?

- Was there a verse that affected you?

- How did you finally come to the point of believing and trusting in Christ?

- How did you receive Jesus (sinner/sacrifice/faith)?

Part III – Life with Christ

- What has happened to you since trusting Christ?

- What kinds of changes were there in your attitudes, motives, goals, and so on?

- What is important to you now, as compared to before?

- Did things change right away, or was it gradual?

- What does your relationship with Jesus mean to you now?

- Is there a verse that means a lot to you today?

Conclusion

- How do you finish strongly and give yourself an exit?

Find printable worksheets of both appendices and all the chapter questions at www.cwdouglas.com/resources.

Made in the USA
Columbia, SC
29 May 2018